Aligning Your CREATIVE SEQUENCE to the Core Music Standards

By Tim Purdum

Published by

Aligning Your Creative Sequence to the Core Music Standards

by
Tim Purdum

© 2014 by Cedar River Music

Cover illustration and design by Benjamin Hitmar. © 2014 by Tim Purdum.
Photographs © 2012-2013 by Carole Fishback. Used by permission.
Images of children in this book were used with the express written permission of their parents.

Conceptual Framework, Anchor Standards, Enduring Understandings, Essential Questions, Artistic Processes, Process Components, and Performance Standards
all © 2014 State Education Agency Directors of Arts Education.
Used with permission. For more information:

> State Education Agency Directors of Arts Education. (2014). National Core Arts Standards. Dover, DE: State Education Agency Directors of Arts Education, on behalf of the National Coalition for Core Arts Standards (NCCAS) www.nationalartsstandards.org

Edited by Alan Purdum and Amy Frohardt-Schafer.

Purchase of this book gives the user permission to use the included lessons for teaching children. All other rights reserved.
For permission requests, contact the publisher.

Cedar River Music
2304 Franklin Street
Cedar Falls, IA 50613
www.cedarrivermusic.com
tim@cedarrivermusic.com

Printed in the United States of America

ISBN 978-0-9859001-6-8

First Edition, 2014

Creative Sequence Titles

Creative Sequence: Teaching Music with Flexibility & Organization

Xylophone & Other Barred Percussion: A Creative Sequence

Recorder: A Creative Sequence

Aligning Your Creative Sequence to the Core Music Standards

Acknowledgements

Thanks go to Cory Wilkerson and the State Education Agency Directors of Arts Education (SEADAE) for permission to print and share part of the new standards. (This does not signify an endorsement of my work, merely permission to use theirs.) Thanks to my father Alan Purdum for his content editing. Thanks to Amy Frohardt-Schafer, our new editor, who understands proper English much better than I do.

Thanks to all of the dedicated teachers who contributed to the new standards and to the ongoing discussion of the standards online. The vibrant voice of music educators is being heard.

Finally, thanks as always to my family, who are very supportive whenever I disappear to write.

Table of Contents

About the Creative Sequence	1
Introduction to the National Core Music Standards	2
What the Core Standards Are	3
What You Need to Know in Order to Understand the Core Standards	6
About the Lessons in this Volume	8
Teaching with the Core Standards Throughout the Year	9
Conceptual Matrix	11
Artistic Processes	11
Anchor Standards, Process Components, Enduring Understanding, and Essential Questions	13
Performance Standards	18
Understanding the Standards Code	18
Artistic Process: Creating	19
Artistic Process: Performing	35
Artistic Process: Responding	62
Artistic Process: Connecting	88
Practical Application	89
Accommodating Reflective Practice	89
Connecting the Artistic Processes	91
Focusing on Skills and Elements	92
Coda	93
Selected Bibliography	94

About the Creative Sequence

Thank you for purchasing **Aligning Your Creative Sequence to the Core Music Standards**. This volume is part of the *Creative Sequence* series, which is designed to aid creative music teachers in developing their own curricula, choosing repertoire, and planning lessons. While the book can certainly be utilized as a stand-alone resource, we highly recommend using it in conjunction with the core *CS* book - **Creative Sequence: Teaching Music with Flexibility and Organization**.

The fundamental philosophy of *CS* is that a quality music education requires more flexibility, differentiation, and personalization on the part of the teacher than is possible by strictly following even a high-quality textbook series. In this series are sample ideas, instructions for how to develop your own lessons, and the tools to organize and deliver this creative instruction. These lessons and ideas can be incorporated into your existing teaching style, repertoire, and curriculum. This volume is focused on the new standards; it should not be interpreted as a comprehensive elementary music sequence by itself. Other **Creative Sequence** volumes deal in greater depth with various media, repertoire, and elements.

__Introduction to the National Core Music Standards__

The Music Educators National Conference (MENC), now the National Association for Music Education (NAfME), along with other national arts educators associations, last published National Standards for Arts Education in 1994. These standards were highly regarded by practicing teachers, and formed the foundation for numerous state standards. There has been interest since then, however, to create more alignment between the various arts, as well as to align these standards with the Common Core standards movement.

In 2009, as the Race to the Top national legislation came out, the State Education Agency Directors of Arts Education (SEADAE), along with representatives from many national arts organizations, began to lay the groundwork for new national arts standards. Over the next two years, this work took clearer shape, as NAfME and the other professional organizations endorsed the idea. Research from the College Board was gathered to help inform the writing process. In 2011, the National Coalition for Core Arts Standards (NCCAS) was formed. There was an open call for writers, and from a pool of over 300 candidates, ten lead writers were selected for each art discipline. It is important to note that none of the ten selected for the lead writing team were practicing elementary music educators. Rather, the group consisted of high school teachers, collegiate professors, and representatives from state education departments. This music team, and the writing teams for the other arts disciplines, began meeting and writing in 2012. To achieve transparency, the NCCAS posted information online at nccas.wikispaces.com.

Once the framework structure was agreed upon between the arts disciplines, larger teams were formed to write performance standards for each discipline and grade level. These teams did include practicing elementary music educators. In July of 2013, the first public draft of these standards was released, along with a survey for the public to provide feedback. Thousands of teachers responded to the online survey, and the writing teams continued working on the document, taking this feedback into account. A second draft was released in March 2014, with the final document being released in June of that same year.

While the process included two public reviews, as well as calls for participants in the early stages, it should be noted that, due to the nature of aligning the various art forms, not all public comments based on the Conceptual Matrix (explained in the next chapter) and overall structure of the standards were able to be honored in the revisions.[1]

What the Core Standards Are

Based on hundreds of hours of personal analysis before, during, and after the review process, this author believes the following points to be true about the new Core Music Standards.

1. *Focused on Process*: The shift from a content and skills format to a process focus is a positive step in identifying how students should learn music. This will hopefully reinforce the shift in general music education over the past half century away from paper-pencil testing, rote memorization of facts, and mechanical performance toward a more holistic, creative approach.

2. *Focused on Critical Thinking*: The vast majority of the Performance Standards in the new Core Standards include the words *explain* or *discuss*. While demonstrating thorough understanding of musical concepts is important, it is this author's belief that a focus on demonstrating understanding through discussion rather than through creative and performance application, can lead to an unbalanced and less-successful musical education. It is imperative that *active music making* remain the primary purpose and activity in music classes, with reflection, discussion, and analysis *serving* the students in their music-making process.

3. *Intentionally Devoid of Content and Skills*: Probably the largest paradigm shift from the 1994 standards to the new Core Standards is the move away from content and skills to an exclusive focus on process. For example, the 1994 standards included the skills of *singing, playing instruments, improvising,*

---

[1] This section is based on information from http://www.dipity.com/National/National-Arts-Standards-2-0-Working-Time-Line, which is no longer an active link.

composing, arranging, reading, notating, listening, analyzing, describing, and *evaluating.* Of these, the new Core Standards only specifically mention *improvising, reading, notating, listening, analyzing, describing,* and *evaluating.* Notice that singing and playing instruments are now referred to by the verb *perform,* leaving room, for better or worse, for teachers to select only instrumental or vocal, if they so choose. Composing and arranging are referred to by the very non-music-specific verbs *generate* and *create.*

For content, the 1994 standards included *Achievement Standards* for grade bands K-4, 5-8, and 9-12. Under the reading and notating standard, 4th graders were expected to know and be able to use "whole, half, dotted half, quarter, and eighth notes and rests in 2/4, 3/4, and 4/4 meter signatures." Similar guidelines were established for pitch notation, dynamics, tempos, and articulation. In the new Core Standards, students are asked to "read and perform using standard notation," but there is no description of which notation elements should be learned and when. When considering the fact that the new Performance Standards are grade-level specific, rather than grade bands, this omission is all the more noticeable.

Since the omission of performance skills and content guidelines was the source of much discussion during the review process, it can only be assumed that this was an intentional absence by design. According to their website, NAfME states:

> These voluntary standards allow a great deal of flexibility for states, districts and teachers to develop unique curriculum. Teachers in the field requested that suggested knowledge and skills be crafted as a supplement to the standards.[2]

In this author's opinion, this statement is not accurate. Many teachers requested that the knowledge and skills be included *in* the new standards, not as a supplement. While this certainly does allow flexibility on the part of teachers with various schedules, class sizes, and materials, it neither helps align the

---

[2] http://musiced.nafme.org/news/the-new-national-core-music-standards-are-out-and-heres-nafme-wants-you-to-know/

education of transient students, nor does it guide teachers in aligning curricula across a district or state. It also potentially could be interpreted to mean that performance skills and content are *less important* than process goals, such as selecting, explaining, and planning.

4. *An Ending Point, Not a Beginning Point*: Despite the focus on process, which should be the driving force behind every lesson, and the lack of skills and elemental concepts, the Core Standards are written in such a way that the process they describe begins with the assumption of a *deep and comprehensive prior experience*. For example, students are asked to select music to respond to or perform. This can only be done if the students have a wide experience of listening and performing from which to draw. For performing, students are expected to analyze a piece of music, yet the basic skills of reading, listening, singing, and playing involved are not explained. In the creating process, students are asked to create new ideas based on their personal interests, but the building blocks, such as rhythms, melodies, and forms, for composition and notation are not explained.

    This point is very important. Teachers, especially beginning teachers, should avoid the temptation to begin teaching the processes described in the Core Standards from Day One. Rather, they should *build their curriculum and lesson plans around learning the elements of music and developing performance, creative, and literacy skills*. Of course, the steps described in the Core Standards can be integrated directly into this skill-building. The danger is in jumping directly to analysis, composition, and reflection too soon, because the *actual musical ability level* of the students will be lessened due to lack of time spent exploring and practicing key skills.

5. *Good Guidelines for Assessment Projects*: As guidelines for semester-end or year-end projects, the new Core Standards really shine. They highlight the high end culminating activities that are possible for students in sequential music classes. They are also flexible enough to be adapted to a variety of student skill levels and experience. The creative-assessment-project lessons written for this

volume are written for this very purpose: to align end-of-course projects with the new Core Standards.

What You Need to Know in Order to Understand the Core Standards

1. *Creativity comes through experience and exposure.* The creative process strand of the Core Standards uses the verbs *create*, *improvise*, and *generate* to describe the first step, *Plan*. For example, MUCr1.1.2a[3] (Second Grade) states, "Improvise rhythmic and melodic patterns and musical ideas for a specific musical purpose." Missing from the standards are references to the repertoire and background experience from which students can draw to create new ideas. A Language Arts analogy would be to ask students to write a complete sentence in a new language with which they are not familiar. Students need a tonal and rhythmic vocabulary of familiar sounds to explore when improvising, and these must be *presented* by the teacher and *performed* by the students before any improvisation can take place.

   Improvisation is a creative application of primarily familiar material that follows after listening and performance in a successful lesson; it is not normally the start of the musical process, as is implied by the layout of the standards. Spontaneous originality does happen, but it is the exception, not the rule, in learning to create new music.

2. *Asking students to select their own music requires both familiarity with quality repertoire and teacher oversight.* When given complete freedom of choice, students will likely choose to perform music with which they are already familiar, such as popular music from the radio. As the *first* step in the performing process strand, *Select* implies that all music should be chosen by the students, and never mentions how to prepare them to make such a selection.

---

[3] See **Conceptual Matrix** for an explanation of the new standard code system.

This is once again both unclear and backwards. The best examples of student-centered choice in elementary ages involve performing and listening to a wide range of quality repertoire (over many class periods, weeks, and even months), and then allowing students the chance to discuss, select, and perform what they feel is the best of the presented music.

Certainly, as students get older, more freedom can be given to allow them to research more music online. However, do we really want to give up the rich folk music historical traditions of the world? Right now, many—if not most—American children do not sing at home or in their community. Their families are not passing down the music that was our birthright for generations before the technological revolution. Instead, modern technology and popular musicians have replaced this *making* music with *listening* to someone else do the work. If we only allow them to study this "popular" music, we reinforce the idea of music as a solo or small-group performance of professionals, rather than a community activity.

3. *Discussion, reflection, and analysis should be proportional to time spent developing musical skills.* Since the vast majority of content standards include higher-order thinking verbs, an inexperienced teacher or administrator could easily arrive at the conclusion that a large portion of classroom time should be spent on such discussions. To use two more analogies, imagine a math classroom where more time was spent discussing theory than practicing problems, or a physical education class where students sat and talked about basketball strategies, rather than playing the game. Like math, phys. ed., and many other school subjects, music is a hands-on activity that is learned primarily through *doing*, not discussing. Reflection and analysis can only exist when there is skilled experience upon which to reflect and analyze. Thus, the teacher's primary role is to facilitate the development of musical skills, which can then inform short discussions.

About the Lessons in this Volume

In writing this volume, the author's primary goal is to provide a clear set of *teacher* guidelines for how to integrate and achieve the National Core Music Standards. Since the new standards can be read as a process of sequential steps in a single project, these lessons were designed as either one cohesive lesson or a group of interconnected activities. This will allow the veteran teacher to tackle these new standards in a limited amount of time, without completely eliminating existing quality lessons and curriculum goals. Since these lessons address the lack of skills and concepts in the Core Standards, beginning teachers can also use them as models to begin building a creative curriculum.

There are certainly many different ways to approach achieving the Core Standards. NCCAS and NAfME have introduced *Model Cornerstone Assessments* (MCA). The MCA are offered for music in Grades 2, 5, 8 and for ensembles. While similar in focus to the lessons in this volume, the MCA have several drawbacks. First, they are incredibly long (for example, the second grade MCA is 22 pages, just for the Performing process); and they are also confusing to read. There is no clear description of the teaching activities that lead up to the assessments. There is a section marked "Instructions: Over the course of the academic year, students...," but this section merely restates the standards themselves. In addition, there are suggested songs, content knowledge, and vocabulary, but no examples of how these are to be taught.

The assessments themselves are well-designed worksheets. At the beginning of the MCA, it is stated that this collection should be used as choices for teachers to select. It is not always clear, however, which sheets are for teachers and which are for students to fill out. The collection is also overwhelming, with ten worksheets in the 2nd Grade Performing MCA alone.

In this volume, the goal is a clear, simple model that leads from teaching to assessment. Rather than offer ten different possibilities that are likely to be confusing to select and implement, this author has chosen to give one approach as a model. Whether or not you choose to follow this exact sequence with your own students, this model will hopefully provide a better picture of the entire process that leads up to, and includes, assessment.

Teaching with the Core Standards Throughout the Year

Since both the Model Cornerstone Assessments and the lessons in this volume focus on goal projects, you should still have a large portion of the school year that is not dedicated to these activities. Here are some guidelines for integrating Core Standards throughout the year.

1. *Most lessons throughout the year should continue to focus on skill-building and knowledge-building.* Despite the heavy emphasis on higher-order thinking skills in the Core Standards, teachers must continue to provide students with quality, hands-on, active music-making experiences. Goals such as singing, playing an instrument, improvising, and understanding and using basic notation should *not* be watered down to make room for reflection and discussion. This will mean that some Core Standards, such as *Create: Imagine, Perform: Analyze, Perform: Rehearse, Evaluate, & Refine*, and *Perform: Present* will have to be the primary focus of many class periods throughout the year. In-depth *Create* processes should be explored as often as possible, but these will not always follow the steps in the Core Standards. *Respond* processes can and should be integrated in a logical fashion with performance and creative activities. Activities such as *selecting* music for response or performance have an important but limited role, and teachers should not let such discussions and projects distract the class from learning new skills and materials.

2. *Not all classroom processes follow the same sequence as the Core Standards.* It is often the case that a performance piece becomes the foundation for creative exploration, and a listening activity becomes the impetus for performance. Creative exploration of music in the elementary classroom does not and should not follow a single stream.

3. *Begin with model creative lessons.* In order to understand how the new standards will have an impact upon your classroom, it is important first to have experience with and resources for teaching creative lessons. You should explore the **Creative Sequence** series, Orff Schulwerk training and workshops, and other available resources. Without a grounding in creative teaching, the Core Standards can potentially lead teachers astray by focusing on higher-order thinking skills and neglecting the performance/creative skills upon which higher-order musical thinking is based.

Conceptual Matrix

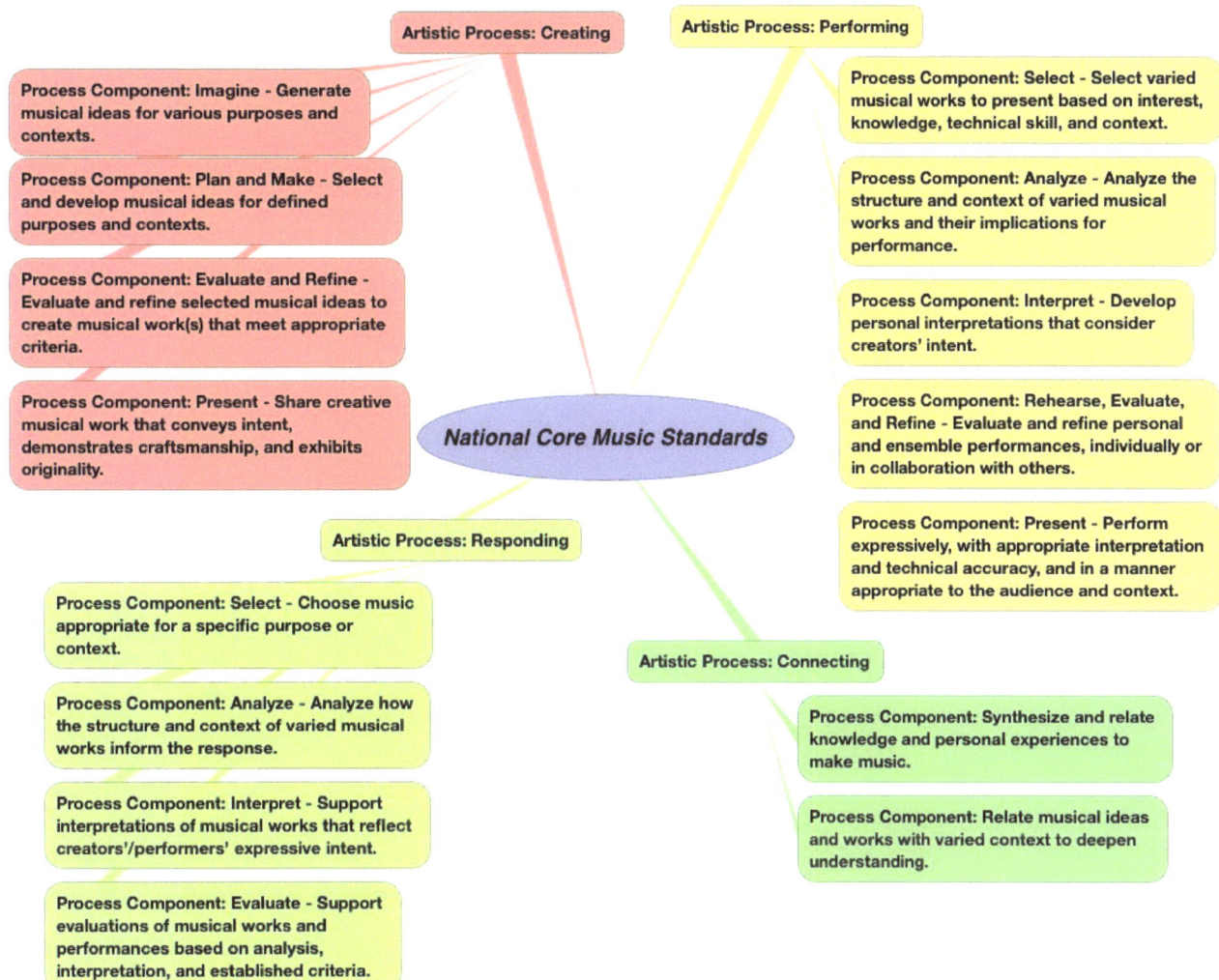

Artistic Processes

There are four Artistic Processes identified as common across the arts disciplines. These were selected as the different ways by which artists and consumers interact with art. By moving away from skills and content to processes, the goal was to better describe the types of activities that would take place in a typical classroom.

Creating

Creating in music education encompasses all exploration, improvisation, composition, and arranging activities. While some would argue that *interpreting* music is also a creative process, this is included in the performing strand since it is considered more a part of that sequence of events. Creating aligns best with the 1994 standards #3 (improvising) and #4 (composing & arranging) and refers to notating (1994 standard #5). It is broken down in the Core Standards into imagine, plan, make, evaluate, refine, and present.

Performing(Presenting/Producing)

While *performing* is the strand in music, drama, and theater, this term aligns with *presenting* for visual arts and *producing* for media arts. Performing in the Core Music Standards refers to the selection, analysis, preparation, practice, presentation, and interpretation of music. It aligns with the 1994 standards #1 (singing), #2 (playing instruments), and #5 (reading & writing).

Responding

Responding refers to the ability to select, analyze, interpret, and evaluate music performed by others, either recorded or live. This corresponds closely to the 1994 standards #6 (listening, responding, & analyzing) and #7 (evaluating).

Connecting

The connecting strand was added after the first draft review. It was an effort to separate and identify ways that the multiple arts could link to each other. Connecting replaces the 1994 standards #8 (connecting to other arts & disciplines) and #9 (connecting to history and culture).

Anchor Standards, Process Components, Enduring Understanding, and Essential Questions

Like the Processes, the Anchor Standards are uniform across the arts. Each art discipline, however, also rewrote the Anchor Standards into discipline-specific *Process Components*. For example, the Anchor Standard "Generate and conceptualize artistic ideas and work" was rewritten as "Generate music ideas for various purposes and context." While each Process Component is written as a full sentence, it is also summarized with one or several words, such as *select*, *plan & make*, or *present*.

Accompanying each Process Component are two sentences that describe the standard. The first is the *Enduring Understanding*, which describes what students should understand about the standard. The second is an *Essential Question*, which is similar to the EU, but in question form.

Creating

Anchor Standard #1: *Generate and conceptualize artistic ideas and work.*

> Process Component: *Imagine* - Generate musical ideas for various purposes and contexts.
>
> - *Enduring Understanding:* The creative ideas, concepts, and feelings that influence musicians' work emerge from a variety of sources.
> - *Essential Question:* How do musicians generate creative ideas?

Anchor Standard #2: *Organize and develop artistic ideas and work.*

> Process Component: *Plan and Make* - Select and develop musical ideas for defined purposes and contexts.
>
> - *Enduring Understanding:* Musicians' creative choices are influenced by their expertise, context, and expressive intent.
> - *Essential Question:* How do musicians make creative decisions?

Anchor Standard #3: *Refine and complete artistic work.*

Process Component: *Creating: Evaluate and Refine* - Evaluate and refine selected musical ideas to create musical work(s) that meet appropriate criteria.

- *Enduring Understanding:* Musicians evaluate, and refine their work through openness to new ideas, persistence, and the application of appropriate criteria.
- *Essential Question:* How do musicians improve the quality of their creative work?

Process Component: *Present* - Share creative musical work that conveys intent, demonstrates craftsmanship, and exhibits originality.

- *Enduring Understanding:* Musicians' presentation of creative work is the culmination of a process of creation and communication.
- *Essential Question:* When is creative work ready to share?

Performing

Anchor Standard #4: *Analyze, interpret, and select artistic work for presentation.*

Process Component: *Select* - Select varied musical works to present based on interest, knowledge, technical skill, and context.

- *Enduring Understanding:* Performers' interest in and knowledge of musical works, understanding of their own technical skill, and the context for a performance influence the selection of repertoire.
- *Essential Question:* How do performers select repertoire?

Process Component: *Analyze* - Analyze the structure and context of varied musical works and their implications for performance.

- *Enduring Understanding:* Analyzing creators' context and how they manipulate elements of music provides insight into their intent and informs performance.
- *Essential Question:* How does understanding the structure and context of musical works inform performance?

Process Component: *Interpret* - Develop personal interpretations that consider creators' intent.

- *Enduring Understanding:* Performers make interpretive decisions based on their understanding of context and expressive intent.
- *Essential Question*: How do performers interpret musical works?

Anchor Standard #5: *Develop and refine artistic work for presentation.*

Process Component: *Rehearse, Evaluate, and Refine* - Evaluate and refine personal and ensemble performances, individually or in collaboration with others.

- *Enduring Understanding:* To express their musical ideas, musicians analyze, evaluate, and refine their performance over time through openness to new ideas, persistence, and the application of appropriate criteria.
- *Essential Question:* How do musicians improve the quality of their performance?

Anchor Standard #6: *Convey meaning through the presentation of artistic work.*

Process Component: *Present* - Perform expressively, with appropriate interpretation and technical accuracy, and in a manner appropriate to the audience and context.

- *Enduring Understanding:* Musicians judge performance based on criteria that vary across time, place, and cultures. The context and how a work is presented influence the audience response.
- *Essential Question:* When is a performance judged ready to present? How do context and the manner in which musical work is presented influence audience response?

Responding

<u>Anchor Standard #7</u>: *Perceive and analyze artistic work.*

<u>Process Component</u>: *Select* - Choose music appropriate for a specific purpose or context.

- *Enduring Understanding:* Individuals' selection of musical works is influenced by their interests, experiences, understandings, and purposes.
- *Essential Question:* How do individuals choose music to experience?

<u>Process Component</u>: *Analyze* - Analyze how the structure and context of varied musical works inform the response.

- *Enduring Understanding:* Response to music is informed by analyzing context (social, cultural, and historical) and how creators and performers manipulate the elements of music.
- *Essential Question:* How does understanding the structure and context of music inform a response?

<u>Anchor Standard #8</u>: *Interpret intent and meaning in artistic work.*

<u>Process Component</u>: *Interpret* - Support interpretations of musical works that reflect creators'/performers' expressive intent.

- *Enduring Understanding:* Through their use of elements and structures of music, creators and performers provide clues to their expressive intent.

- *Essential Question:* How do we discern the musical creators' and performers' expressive intent?

Anchor Standard #9: Apply criteria to evaluate artistic work.

Process Component: Evaluate - Support evaluations of musical works and performances based on analysis, interpretation, and established criteria.

- *Enduring Understanding:* The personal evaluation of musical work(s) and performance(s) is informed by analysis, interpretation, and established criteria.
- *Essential Question:* How do we judge the quality of musical work(s) and performance(s)?

Connecting

Anchor Standard #10: Synthesize and relate knowledge and personal experiences to make music.

- *Enduring Understanding:* Musicians connect their personal interests, experiences, ideas, and knowledge to creating, performing, and responding.
- *Essential Question:* How do musicians make meaningful connections to creating, performing, and responding?

Anchor Standard #11: Relate musical ideas and works with varied context to deepen understanding.

- *Enduring Understanding:* Understanding connections to varied contexts and daily life enhances musicians' creating, performing, and responding
- *Essential Question:* How do the other arts, other disciplines, contexts, and daily life inform creating, performing, and responding to music?

Performance Standards

Beneath each Process Component, there is a Performance Standard written for each individual grade level (PreK-8 for the General Music Standards). Often, the Performance Standard is nearly identical from one grade to the next, with only one or two words changed to demonstrate a more advanced task. Verbs such as *demonstrate* and *describe* appear more often in the lower grades, while more challenging cognitive tasks, such as *explain*, are prevalent in the upper grades. The Performance Standards are written into the *National/State Standards* box for each lesson plan in the following chapters.

Understanding the Standards Code

The new Core Standards are initially organized by art discipline ("MU" for music) and *Process* strand ("Cr" for Creating, "Pr" for Performing, and "Re" for Responding). The first number to follow the process code refers to the *Anchor Standard*. Thus, a 1 under *Performing* refers to the *Select* standard. The second number is for the *Process Component* related to that Anchor Standard. The final number (or letter) refers to the grade level.

Example	Discipline	Process	Anchor Standard	Process Component	Grade
MU:Cr3.1.2	MU (Music)	Cr (Creating)	3 (Refine and complete artistic work)	1 (Present)	2 (Second Grade)

The main website for the National Core Arts Standards (nationalartsstandards.org) includes many excellent tools for analyzing and studying the standards and understanding their organization.

Artistic Process: Creating

The creative process should be an ongoing part of every music class. Seeds of ideas that germinate from listening examples or performance repertoire become the starting point for improvisation and composition. Classroom, group, or individual arranging and interpretation of performance material is likewise a creative endeavor.

Due to the alignment of varying art disciplines, however, the Creating Process strand of the National Core Standards is presented in a similar way to a visual arts project; each piece is a step in a longer process. Such thorough musical activities, which result in well-planned compositions, are rewarding yet time consuming. While shorter improvisation and compositional activities should occur throughout the year, this author recommends that these larger, comprehensive projects occur only a few times each year. The lesson plans below were written with these large projects in mind.

The level of difficulty on any given project may or may not be appropriate for your students. You may freely rearrange activities and ideas from one grade to the next. In particular, the fourth-grade lesson is potentially more musically challenging than the fifth-grade lesson. They are presented this way to allow the older students more personal expression and freedom.

	Creating Strand - Kindergarten
Grade/Class	Kindergarten
Date	Middle to end of the school year
<u>**Primary Elemental Objective**</u>	**Form:** Create and document an original sound poem that tells a story, with a beginning, middle, and ending.
Secondary Elemental Objectives	**Melody**: Explore vocal range and melodic direction through sound effects to accompany a story. **Rhythm**: Explore steady beat to accompany a story. **Expression**: Explore loud/soft and fast/slow opposites while creating sound effects to accompany a story.

National/State Standards	**Core Music Standards:**
	MU:Cr1.1.K
	a. With guidance, explore and experience music concepts (such as beat and melodic contour).
	b. With guidance, generate musical ideas (such as movements or motives).
	MU:Cr2.1.K
	a. With guidance, demonstrate and choose favorite musical ideas.
	b. With guidance, organize personal musical ideas using iconic notation and/or recording technology.
	MU:Cr3.1.K
	   With guidance, apply personal, peer, and teacher feedback in refining personal musical ideas.
	MU:Cr3.2.K
	   With guidance, demonstrate a final version of personal musical ideas to peers.
		21st Century Skills:
		• Creativity & Innovation
		• Critical Thinking & Problem Solving
		• Communication & Collaboration
		• Flexibility & Adaptability
		• Initiative & Self-Direction
		• Productivity & Accountability
		• Leadership & Responsibility

<u>**Repertoire**</u>	Picture Books	
<u>**Media**</u>	Vocal Sounds Instrumental Sounds	Movement

	Creating Strand - Kindergarten
Process **- Experience** **- Analyze** **- Create**	*Prior Knowledge & Skills* • Identify and perform steady beat, high/low vocal sounds, and loud/soft contrasts. • Explore, identify, and understand proper use and care of unpitched percussion instruments. *Imagine* 1. Read a storybook to the class, and ask them to add sound effects to the story. Encourage exploration, and look for chances to add beat, high/low melodic contours, loud/soft, and other expressive ideas. 2. Repeat this process with new stories. In addition to sound effects, explore movement ideas and instrumental effects (such as hand drums and shakers). 3. Guide the class in drawing graphic representations of various sound and movement ideas on the board. Ask for suggestions, and review the ideas that came up during the storytelling. *Plan and Make* 4. Choose a new story, and read it to the class. Rather than have students improvise sounds, ask them to make suggestions, and draw their graphic ideas onto the board. Give each student a chance to make a suggestion to add to the story. 5. Assign roles, and test out the story performance. *Evaluate and Refine* 6. After the first performance, go around the room again, and ask each student to give feedback on something he/she really enjoyed, as well as make a suggestion for changing/improving. Repeat the performance and discussion two or three times until the class is satisfied with the project. *Present* 7. Perform the final story through sound and movement for an audience, or video record the class performance so that they can watch it.
Performance Assessment	Check for understanding of graphic notation, roles in the performance, and individual participation in the creative process.

During the course of first grade, students should experience creative activities utilizing both melodic and rhythmic concepts. Since the concepts can be new and challenging for first-grade students, it is helpful to split these into separate lessons. The lesson provided here focuses on rhythm.

Notice also that, while students may perform and analyze using standard notation in first grade, it is perfectly acceptable for the creative application of notation to be delayed until second grade or later.

	Creating Strand - First Grade	
Grade/Class	First Grade	
Date	Middle to end of the school year	
Primary Elemental Objective	**Expression:** Create an original composition that tells a story through use of rhythms, dynamics, vocal inflection, and timbres.	
Secondary Elemental Objectives	**Rhythm**: Explore, improvise, and compose using natural word rhythms. Document using words and/or graphic notation.	
National/State Standards	**Core Music Standards:** MU:Cr1.1.1 a. With limited guidance, create musical ideas (such as answering a musical question) for a specific purpose. MU:Cr2.1.1 a. With limited guidance, demonstrate and discuss personal reasons for selecting musical ideas that represent expressive intent. b. With limited guidance, use iconic or standard notation and/or recording technology to document and organize personal musical ideas. MU:Cr3.1.1 With limited guidance, discuss and apply personal, peer, and teacher feedback to refine personal musical ideas. MU:Cr3.2.1 With limited guidance, convey expressive intent for a specific purpose by presenting a final version of personal musical ideas to peers or informal audience.	**21st Century Skills:** • Creativity & Innovation • Critical Thinking & Problem Solving • Communication & Collaboration • Flexibility & Adaptability • Initiative & Self-Direction • Productivity & Accountability • Leadership & Responsibility
Repertoire	Student-generated content based on a school theme.	
Media	Speech Unpitched Percussion	Body Percussion Movement

Creating Strand - First Grade

Process **- Experience** **- Analyze** **- Create**	*Prior Knowledge & Skills* • Experience and perform rhythmic word chants over a steady beat. *Imagine* 1. Choose a particular theme for the class to explore, based on a holiday, topic from the general classroom, or other important part of the students' lives. Examples could include Earth Day, Hispanic Heritage Month, or dinosaurs (science). Discuss the topic with the class. 2. Ask the class first to brainstorm, then actively explore musical ideas to go along with the topic. For example, a study of weather could focus on sounds for rain, thunder, and wind. A dinosaur unit could focus on stomping feet and growling sounds. Explore loud/soft, high/low, fast/slow, and various vocal, body, and instrumental timbres. 3. Explore movement ideas to express the ideas in the subject. 4. Also guide students to explore word chain chants from the vocabulary associated with the topic, such as "*allosaur, velociraptor, stegosaurus, T-rex!*" *Plan and Make* 5. Split the class into pairs, and assign a specific part of the topic (certain dinosaur, type of weather, etc.) around which to plan a performance. Ask each pair to use two or more expressive sounds and a word chain or movement piece in their performance. Demonstrate one for the class before giving them time to work on their own. Discuss form: Does it start with a sound, then go to the chant, or vice-versa? Both at the same time or separate? 6. As the partners work, move around the room, and ask guiding questions about why they chose specific sounds. Help the groups use graphic notation, and write down the words they chose for their chant. *Evaluate and Refine* 7. Ask each pair to share their ideas/creation with another group. The second group should watch, listen, and provide both positive comments ("What did they do well?") and suggestions ("What would you like to see?") Switch roles, and have the second group perform. 8. Give pairs time to work with the feedback and modify their performances. *Present* 9. Combine the group performances into a rondo or other loosely-connected large performance. Share with an audience or video record for the class to watch.
Performance Assessment	Check for each student participating with his or her partner. Assess students based on their discussion of ideas and performance.

	Creating Strand - Second Grade	
Grade/Class	Second Grade	
Date	Middle to end of the school year	
<u>**Primary Elemental Objective**</u>	**Melody:** Improvise, or compose and perform an original melody in F-*do* Pentatonic.	
Secondary Elemental Objectives	**Form:** Improvise, or compose and perform an original melody in an elemental phrase form (e.g., *aaba, abab, aabb, aaab*).	
National/State Standards	**Core Music Standards:** *MU:Cr1.1.2* a. Improvise rhythmic and melodic patterns and musical ideas for a specific purpose. b. Generate musical patterns and ideas within the context of a given tonality (such as major and minor) and meter (such as duple and triple). *MU:Cr2.1.2* a. Demonstrate and explain personal reasons for selecting patterns and ideas for music that represent expressive intent. b. Use iconic or standard notation and/or recording technology to combine, sequence, and document personal musical ideas. *MU:Cr3.1.2* Interpret and apply personal, peer, and teacher feedback to revise personal music. *MU:Cr3.2.2* Convey expressive intent for a specific purpose by presenting a final version of personal musical ideas to peers or informal audience.	**21st Century Skills:** • Creativity & Innovation • Critical Thinking & Problem Solving • Communication & Collaboration • Flexibility & Adaptability • Initiative & Self-Direction • Productivity & Accountability • Leadership & Responsibility
<u>**Repertoire**</u>	Any traditional folk song or children's game with an elemental phrase form.	
<u>**Media**</u>	Singing & Speech Barred Percussion	Unpitched & Body Percussion Movement

Creating Strand - Second Grade

Process
- Experience
- Analyze
- Create
	Prior Knowledge & Skills
	• Identify, read, and perform melodies in F-*do* Pentatonic.
	• Identify, read, and perform simple rhythm patterns, including quarter notes, eighth notes, and quarter rests.
	Imagine
	1. Review the F-*do* Pentatonic scale in sight-singing, in solfege, and on barred percussion. Play and sing familiar songs in F-*do* Pentatonic. Identify or review the concept of *tonic* as the most important note (melodies should start on it, end on it, and/or play it a lot), and identify F-*do* as tonic.
	2. Using familiar rhythms, play short phrases in F-*do* Pentatonic on the barred percussion, and ask the class to echo. Next, use a *Question & Answer* format to have students begin to improvise original patterns. Play an 8-beat phrase for the class, then ask the students to "answer" with a different 8-beat phrase. The goal is to borrow ideas without making it an exact echo. Later, split the class into pairs, and have them take turns playing Q&A patterns with their partners. *Question* phrases should start on tonic, while *answer* phrases should end on tonic.
	Plan and Make
	3. Review how to play and sing a model folk song or children's game in a simple phrase form, such as *aaba*, *abab*, *aabb*, or *aaab*. When the class has identified the phrase form, ask them to improvise only the *b* phrase, after you improvise the *a* phrase. Point out that repetitions should be recognizable, but small variations are acceptable (for example, *b′* — "b prime"). The final phrase should end on tonic. Next, switch roles, and have the class improvise an *a* phrase to your *b* phrase.
	4. Give students adequate time to practice and plan their ideas for both *a* and *b* phrases, and to practice playing an entire four-phrase improvisation or memorized composition.
	Evaluate and Refine
	5. Ask the students to reflect silently on their independent work. Use a visual checklist on the board to identify the following goals:
	   • the phrase form is clear, and repetitions are audible
	   • the melody ends on F-*do*
	   • two hands are used alternating
	   • only one note at a time is played (melody)
	   • the melody consists mainly of stepwise motion and repeated notes, with few large leaps
	6. After more practice time, have each student perform his or her piece for the class. Ask other students to give positive comments as well as suggestions to each student. Provide your own feedback as well.
	Present
	7. Give one more practice session after the feedback, and then ask the students to each perform one more time. Create a rondo, using the original folk song, interspersed with student improvisations/compositions. For the sake of length, it works well to hear four students between each folk song repeat. It is acceptable to use four-beat transitions as well, such as "Danny's turn, ready go!" Video record the performance.

Performance Assessment	Assess each student's final performance based on the checklist provided above in step 5.

	Creating Strand - Third Grade	
Grade/Class	Third Grade	
Date	Middle to end of the school year	
Primary Elemental Objective	**Melody:** Compose and notate an original melody in C-*do* Pentatonic, selecting and applying familiar pitches in the first octave of the barred percussion and singing range.	
Secondary Elemental Objectives	**Rhythm:** Compose and notate an original melody, selecting and applying a simple time signature and familiar rhythms. **Form:** Select and apply an elemental phrase form to an original composition.	
National/State Standards	**Core Music Standards:** *MU:Cr1.1.3* a. Improvise rhythmic and melodic ideas, and describe connection to specific purpose and context (such as personal and social). b. Generate musical ideas (such as rhythms and melodies) within a given tonality and/or meter. *MU:Cr2.1.3* a. Demonstrate selected musical ideas for a simple improvisation or composition to express intent, and describe connection to a specific purpose and context. b. Use standard and/or iconic notation and/or recording technology to document personal rhythmic and melodic musical ideas. *MU:Cr3.1.3* Evaluate, refine, and document revisions to personal musical ideas, applying teacher-provided and collaboratively-developed criteria and feedback. *MU:Cr3.2.3* Present the final version of personal created music to others, and describe connection to expressive intent.	**21st Century Skills:** • Creativity & Innovation • Critical Thinking & Problem Solving • Communication & Collaboration • Flexibility & Adaptability • Initiative & Self-Direction • Productivity & Accountability • Leadership & Responsibility
Repertoire	Student-generated content	
Media	Singing & Speech Barred Percussion	Unpitched & Body Percussion Movement

Creating Strand - Third Grade

Process
- **Experience**
- **Analyze**
- **Create**

Prior Knowledge & Skills
- Read and identify quarter notes, eighth note pairs, quarter rests, half notes, dotted half notes, and whole notes in context of familiar songs.
- Read and identify simple time signatures, such as 2/4, 3/4, and 4/4, and perform music in these meters.
- Identify and experience elemental phrase forms in familiar music and nursery rhymes.
- Read and identify C-*do* Pentatonic melodic notes on the treble staff and with hand signs, and perform both vocally and with barred percussion.

Imagine
1. Using rhythm cards (quarter note, quarter rest, 2-eighth notes, half note, dotted half note, whole note) or a writing surface and tool (such as dry-erase boards and markers), ask the students to explore and create various short rhythmic motives of 4-, 6-, and 8-beat lengths. Review the concept of time signatures, and ask what time signatures would correspond to these rhythms, if each pattern represented two measures (2/4, 3/4, 4/4).
2. Show and perform ideas in small groups, and discuss why certain rhythmic ideas were chosen. Explore ideas of difficulty, surprise, repetition, and the emotional feel of different meters.

Plan and Make
3. Have each student select or create one new rhythmic motive, which can be two measures in any of the above meters. Give each student writing tools to notate their ideas.
4. Ask the students, with the help of a partner (who must be writing in the same meter), to practice clapping their rhythms. As the pairs compare their two patterns, have them choose an elemental phrase form (such as *aaba, aabb, abab, aaab*), using one student's motive for the *a* phrase, and the other for the *b* phrase. Ask them to practice the complete rhythmic theme together.
5. Once each group has performed and shown their notated pattern to you, ask them to move to the barred percussion, set up in C-*do* Pentatonic, and set the rhythm to a melodic line. Review the following guidelines with the class:
   - end on tonic, and reinforce it within the piece
   - make the dominant (*so*) the second most important pitch
   - use primarily stepwise motion and repeated notes
   - make the *a* and *b* phrases distinct
   - create a melody that matches the emotional intent of the rhythmic theme
6. When the partners have created a melody, ask them to notate the melody with note heads on a treble clef staff. Once you have checked this for accuracy, have them add the rhythmic stems and beams to their melodies.

Evaluate and Refine
7. Group each pair of students with one or two other pairs, and have them present their pieces for each other. Ask the listening groups to give positive comments and constructive suggestions. Have students assist each other with notating or performance difficulties. As students work, circulate around the room, and look for places where more suggestions are needed.

Present
8. Have each pair of students present their melody to the class. While one group performs, ask the rest of the class to write down their favorite part of each performance, as well as something they wished they had heard.
9. Give each pair a chance to explain to the class the work process that led them to their final product. After they have spoken, allow other students to share their written ideas with the performers.

	Creating Strand - Third Grade
Performance Assessment	*Composition* - Rhythmic motives are simple, clear, and musical. - Phrase form is clear. - Melody follows rules to establish *do* as tonic. *Notation* - Rhythms are accurate and legible. - Barlines and time signatures are accurate. - Melody is accurate and legible. *Performance* - Rhythms and pitches are accurate to the score. - Partners are in time with each other.

	Creating Strand - Fourth Grade	
Grade/Class	Fourth Grade	
Date	Middle to end of the school year	
Primary Elemental Objective	**Melody:** Compose and perform an original melody, using the major scale, with *fa* and *ti* as passing tones.	
Secondary Elemental Objectives	**Rhythm:** Compose an original melody using familiar rhythms, and create at least one complementary rhythmic ostinato part. **Form:** Use phrase forms and a large section form, such as ABA, in composing a melody. **Harmony:** Create a simple drone-based accompaniment for the song, including a complementary melodic ostinato.	

National/State Standards	**Core Music Standards:**
	MU:Cr1.1.4
	a. Improvise rhythmic, melodic, and harmonic ideas, and explain connection to specific purpose and context (such as social and cultural).
	b. Generate musical ideas (such as rhythms, melodies, and simple accompaniment patterns) within related tonalities (such as major and minor) and meters.
	MU:Cr2.1.4
	a. Demonstrate selected and organized musical ideas for an improvisation, arrangement, or composition to express intent, and explain connection to purpose and context.
	b. Use standard and/or iconic notation and/or recording technology to document personal rhythmic, melodic, and simple harmonic musical ideas.
	MU:Cr3.1.4
	    Evaluate, refine, and document revisions to personal music, applying teacher-provided and collaboratively-developed criteria and feedback to show improvement over time.
	MU:Cr3.2.4
	    Present the final version of personal created music to others, and explain connection to expressive intent.
		21st Century Skills:
		• Creativity & Innovation
		• Critical Thinking & Problem Solving
		• Communication & Collaboration
		• Flexibility & Adaptability
		• Initiative & Self-Direction
		• Productivity & Accountability
		• Leadership & Responsibility

Creating Strand - Fourth Grade

Repertoire	Student-generated content

Jubilate Deo
M. Praetorius

Ju - bi - la - te De - o, ju - bi - la - te De - o, Al - le - lu - ia!

Media	Singing & Speech Barred Percussion & Recorder	Unpitched & Body Percussion Movement

Process
- Experience
- Analyze
- Create

Prior Knowledge & Skills
- Read and identify various rhythmic patterns, including sixteenth notes, in familiar music.
- Experience and identify music in large sectional forms, such as ABA or rondo.
- Read, identify, and perform *fa* and *ti* as melodic passing tones in a drone-based song, with both *do* and *la* as tonic.
- Read and understand the parts of a multi-voiced score.

Imagine
1. Teach or review the song "Jubilate Deo." Ask the class to sing in a three-part round. Looking at the staff notation, identify the solfege, and point out how the strong beats highlight the tonic chord, while *fa* and *ti* are only used as passing or neighbor tones between beats.
2. Transfer the melody of "Jubilate Deo" to barred percussion. After exploring the complete melody, have the bass xylophone (or lowest instrument in your ensemble) continue to repeat the final phrase of the song.
3. Over the top of this broken drone, have the rest of the class improvise melodies that use *fa* and *ti* as passing tones, and focus on *do*, *mi*, and *so* on strong beats. *Re* and *la* can occur on any beat, but point out that they don't reinforce the tonic as well as the triad tones. Ask students to use sixteenth notes and other familiar rhythms.
4. As students explore ideas, remind them of the use of repetition in phrase forms, such as *abab* or *aaba*. Ask the students to create a 4-phrase pattern using a form with repetition.
5. Have small groups or soloists take turns improvising over the major scale so that individual ideas can be explored and heard. Lead a group discussion about what decisions were made, and compare different ideas from around the class. Discuss how different melodic, rhythmic, and form choices can affect the mood and feeling of an improvisation.

Plan and Make
6. Split the class into small groups of 4-6 students. Discuss the upcoming assignment, and explain that every student will be expected to contribute to each stage in the composing, arranging, and performing process.
7. Assign each group the task of creating two separate 4-phrase pieces. Each piece should be created to represent a specific mood, idea, or theme, and the two should be contrasting. Students can select any familiar meter, with either *do* or *la* as tonic. Give students paper, dry-erase boards, tablets, or other materials to document their composition ideas. This can include recording technology. The goal at this point is for the students to record (in writing or audio) their ideas, not to create perfect traditional notation. One possible system to recommend is rhythmic lines with pitch letter-names written below each note. Be sure, however, that students start first with playing, not writing. Music that is written first, before being heard, is normally not as easy or pleasing as that which is created through sound.
8. Ask students to practice their two pieces, and combine them to make a larger ABA sectional piece. Discuss how to choose which piece becomes the opening/closing (A) and which piece becomes the center (B).

Creating Strand - Fourth Grade

Process (continued)	*Evaluate and Refine*
	9. Have each group perform for the class or for another group. Ask the listeners to give positive feedback and constructive comments for development. As students work and share, move around, and provide teacher feedback as well.
	10. As students refine their melodies based on peer and teacher feedback, each melody should be laid out carefully on a treble clef staff, using paper, dry-erase boards, or technology. Have each group leave three staves empty below the melody. Review concepts such as meter, barlines, stem directions, and other issues that may need to be addressed.
	Plan and Make
	11. Once the longer piece is composed and can be performed, each group or individual should next compose three accompaniment parts: a drone, a rhythmic ostinato, and a melodic ostinato. Each part should have its own complementary rhythm.
	    a. The drone should focus on tonic and fifth, and it should be very simple. Varieties could include a chord drone, broken drone, crossover/arpeggiated drone, or level drone.
	    b. The rhythmic ostinato should be written for an unpitched instrument and should focus on complementary rhythm against the melody.
	    c. The melodic ostinato should focus on the tones of the Pentatonic scale. *Fa* and *ti* should only be used, if at all, as passing tones. Again, the focus should be on simplicity.
	Evaluate and Refine
	12. As students present their written compositions and practice their performances, guide them to find improved harmonies and complementary rhythms.
	Present
	13. Each group will perform their arrangement for the class with one or more students on each part. Performances can be recorded for assessment and sharing purposes. Each group will also turn in a written score, and each student will write a short reflection describing the creative process followed.

Performance Assessment	*Group Composition* - Melodic composition follows rules of drone-based major melody. - Melodic composition follows rules of phrase form repetition and has an ABA sectional form. - Drone reinforces tonic and dominant tones. - Rhythmic ostinato features complementary rhythms. - Melodic ostinato features interesting but not dissonant (half-step) harmonies. *Group Notation* - Pitches are notated accurately. - Rhythms, measures, and barlines are notated accurately. - Parts are aligned vertically. *Group Performance* - Individual parts can be heard. - Starting and stopping are rehearsed and clear. *Individual Composition Contribution* - Student participates with teammates. - Student provides thematic, melodic, rhythmic, and/or harmonic ideas. - Student assists in notating the composition. *Individual Performance Contribution* - Student performs his/her own part with accurate rhythm and pitches, in time with the ensemble. *Individual Feedback & Reflection* - Student provides constructive feedback to others either within his/her group or in another group. - Student accepts feedback to her/his own ideas. - Student can describe his/her own thought-process and contributions to the project.

	Creating Strand - **Fifth Grade**	
Grade/Class	Fifth Grade	
Date	Middle to end of the school year	
<u>Primary Elemental Objective</u>	**Melody:** Write lyrics, set lyrics to music using familiar major or minor scale pitches, notate the melody on the treble staff, and perform the song.	
Secondary Elemental Objectives	**Rhythm:** With teacher assistance, notate the word rhythms of the original song, using both familiar and new rhythmic symbols as needed. **Form:** Use verse, chorus, intro, coda, and optional bridge to create a final performance of the song. **Harmony:** Create a simple chordal harmonic accompaniment for the song, including at least three chords.	

National/State Standards	**Core Music Standards:**
	MU:Cr1.1.5
	a. *Improvise rhythmic, melodic, and harmonic ideas, and explain connection to specific purpose and context (such as social, cultural, and historical).*
	b. *Generate musical ideas (such as rhythms, melodies, and accompaniment patterns) within specific related tonalities, meters, and simple chord changes.*
	MU:Cr2.1.5
	a. *Demonstrate selected and developed musical ideas for improvisations, arrangements, or compositions to express intent, and explain connection to purpose and context.*
	b. *Use standard and/or iconic notation and/or recording technology to document personal rhythmic, melodic, and two-chord harmonic musical ideas.*
	MU:Cr3.1.5
	   Evaluate, refine, and document revisions to personal music, applying teacher-provided and collaboratively-developed criteria and feedback, and explain rationale for changes.
	MU:Cr3.2.5
	   Present the final version of personal created music to others that demonstrates craftsmanship, and explain connection to expressive intent.
		21st Century Skills:
		• Creativity & Innovation
		• Critical Thinking & Problem Solving
		• Communication & Collaboration
		• Flexibility & Adaptability
		• Initiative & Self-Direction
		• Productivity & Accountability
		• Leadership & Responsibility

<u>Repertoire</u>	Student-generated content	
<u>Media</u>	Singing & Speech Barred Percussion & Recorder	Unpitched & Body Percussion Movement

Creating Strand - Fifth Grade

Process
- **Experience**
- **Analyze**
- **Create**

Prior Knowledge & Skills
- Read and identify advanced rhythmic patterns in natural, speech-centered popular music.
- Listen to and identify the structural elements of popular music, such as intro, verse, chorus, bridge, and coda.
- Read and perform diatonic melodies that require harmonic changes.
- Read and perform harmonic chords to accompany a song.

Imagine
1. After listening to and performing several songs with a popular style, have a class discussion about lyrics and the impact they have on the listener.
2. In small groups or as individuals, students should select a story theme and brainstorm words that go with this theme. For each important word identified, students should also seek to find a rhyming word.

Plan and Make
3. Next, students or groups take their brainstormed ideas and begin writing a chorus for a song. The chorus should include the most important themes that will be repeated throughout the piece. It should be a clear, defined length, such as four lines, and, if possible, it should rhyme.
4. Once the chorus lyrics are written, they should be spoken in rhythm. Students should use an audio recording device to document their choices. Assist students in transferring rhythms to standard notation. (Natural speech flow may include rhythms beyond the written experience of elementary students.)

Imagine
5. Using their voices and melodic/harmonic instruments, students should explore melodic ideas to fit their chorus. This can be done freely at first, using their ear and singing voices, and then checked against an instrument for pitch and implied harmonies.

Plan and Make
6. Next, students will begin selecting and notating their melodic ideas. A key and tonic should be selected, and the melody should be notated on the treble staff.
7. Using a harmonic instrument, such as keyboard, ukulele, guitar, or xylophone, students should identify the implied harmonies that occur on strong beats in the melody (for example, *re* or *ti* implies a V chord, *fa* or *la* implies a IV chord in major), and write in Roman numeral or chord names above the melody.

Evaluate and Refine
8. Once the chorus is complete with chordal accompaniment, students should present it for their peers and you. Positive feedback and constructive ideas should be shared, and students should take these ideas and continue to refine the chorus.
9. Steps 3-8 should be repeated for writing verses to the song. Each verse after the first should follow the same harmonic and melodic patterns, with only minor variations in rhythms as necessary to fit the text.
10. With your assistance and that of their peers, students should create an instrumental introduction, coda, and optional bridge for the song.
11. Additional harmonic or rhythmic parts (e.g., drums) can be added, if desired.

Present
12. Final presentations can be for a live audience or video/audio recorded.

	Creating Strand - Fifth Grade
Performance Assessment	*Lyric Writing* - Lyrics are topical to a theme and have a regular phrase length with some rhyming. - Lyrics are divided into clear verse and chorus. *Rhythmic, Melodic, & Harmonic Writing* - Rhythms are notated accurately. - Melodic composition follows rules of major melody and chord-based harmonies. - Melodic composition follows rules of verse/chorus form, including repetition. - Chords reinforce melodic tones on strong beats, and follow a clear pattern. *Group Notation* - Pitches are notated accurately. - Rhythms, measures, and barlines are notated accurately. - Chords align vertically with the melody. *Group Performance* - Balance is heard between melody and chordal accompaniment. - Starting and stopping are rehearsed and clear. *Individual Composition Contribution* - Student participates with teammates. - Student provides thematic, melodic, rhythmic, and/or harmonic ideas. - Student assists in notating the composition. *Individual Performance Contribution* - Student performs his/her own part with accurate rhythm and pitches, in time with the ensemble. *Individual Feedback & Reflection* - Student provides constructive feedback to others either within his/her group or in another group. - Student accepts feedback to her/his own ideas. - Student can describe his/her own thought-process and contributions to the project.

Artistic Process: Performing

Performance is both the foundation and the *goal* of a strong music education program. Music has always been a part of being human, and making music is the purest musical experience. Improvisation, while listed separately here, is really spontaneous performance, and composition is simply preparing new music for performance. While listening to music is important, it is a secondary activity when compared to *making* music.

With the focus on analytical skills in the new Core Standards, it would be easy to spend too much time analyzing, discussing, and reflecting. Whenever possible, therefore, such activities should be limited in scope and time. In the younger grades, discussions should be informal and verbal, as many students lack the writing skills to document their thoughts quickly. Even when you are working with older students, consider using some form of multiple-choice worksheets to assess certain understandings, and give your students only a handful of longer written assignments, perhaps one to five per year. Remember that the goal of student performance is *immersion in making music*, not discussion or reflection.

In the original, cross-discipline Anchor Standard, the wording suggests that the *selection* of artwork occurs *after* analysis and interpretation, not before as is suggested by the Process Components in the Music Standards. Given that students must be exposed to quality repertoire in order to make informed decisions, this author has placed Select *after* Analyze in the lesson process.

Repertoire suggestions were not made for the Performing process, as these should reflect the existing curriculum of your program. The **Creative Sequence** series offers several volumes (with more to come), containing grade-specific repertoire choices.

	Performing Strand - **Kindergarten**	
Grade/Class	Kindergarten	
Date	Full Year	
<u>**Primary Elemental Objective**</u>	**Rhythm**: Perform the steady beat through a variety of media.	
Secondary Elemental Objectives	**Melody**: Identify melodic line and explore singing voice to match pitch. **Expression**: Explore expressive opposites such as loud/soft and fast/slow through a variety of media. **Style**: Perform traditional children's songs/games and folk materials.	

National/State Standards	**Core Music Standards:**
	MU:Pr4.1.K
	    With guidance, demonstrate and state personal interest in varied musical selections.
	MU:Pr4.2.K
	    With guidance, explore and demonstrate awareness of music contrasts (such as high/low, loud/soft, same/different) in a variety of music selected for performance.
	MU:Pr4.3.K
	    With guidance, demonstrate awareness of expressive qualities (such as voice quality, dynamics, and tempo) that support the creators' expressive intent.
	MU:Pr5.1.K
	a. *With guidance, apply personal, teacher, and peer feedback to refine performances.*
	b. *With guidance, use suggested strategies in rehearsal to improve the expressive qualities of music.*
	MU:Pr6.1.K
	a. *With guidance, perform music with expression.*
	b. *Perform appropriately for the audience.*
		21st Century Skills:
		• Critical Thinking & Problem Solving
		• Communication & Collaboration
		• Flexibility & Adaptability
		• Initiative & Self-Direction
		• Productivity & Accountability
		• Leadership & Responsibility

	Performing Strand - Kindergarten	
<u>Repertoire</u>	Current existing curricular repertoire.	
<u>Media</u>	Singing & Speech Unpitched Percussion	Body Percussion Movement

<u>Process</u>
<u>- Experience</u>
<u>- Analyze</u>
<u>- Create</u>
	Prior Knowledge & Skills
	• Maintain a steady beat.
	• Find upper register singing voice, and match pitch with a vocal model.
	Analyze
	1. Lead the class in a variety of simple singing games, such as "I'm a Little Teapot," "The Itsy-Bitsy Spider," "London Bridge," and "The Ants Go Marching." At the beginning of the year, you are leading the songs, and the students are playing the games. As time progresses, ask and encourage students to sing along or even sing without your help.
	2. Select appropriate songs to identify various contrasting ideas.
	   a. high/low - "Over in the Meadow"
	   b. loud/soft - "The Other Day (I Met a Bear)"
	   c. fast/slow - "Engine Engine Number Nine"
	Interpret
	3. Encourage students to use their voices expressively to demonstrate the contrasting ideas listed above. As appropriate, discuss the meaning of the song lyrics, and the impact that loud/soft and fast/slow choices have on a performance.
	Select
	4. After a wide variety of traditional songs have been introduced and sung in class, lead a class discussion of favorite songs. This could occur before the school concert, allowing the students to give input on which songs should be performed.
	5. Use a "vote" system, such as multiple buckets with an image related to a song on each one. Give students 1-4 sticks to place in the buckets. Tally the results in that class and across the grade, and share the results with the students.
	Rehearse, Evaluate, and Refine
	6. As familiar songs are practiced throughout the year, give students multiple opportunities to sing short phrases alone as echo-patterns. Give each child immediate positive and constructive feedback on pitch-matching, breath, and projection. Be sure to accept any attempt (or none) at first, and only gradually increase the amount of constructive help you give, after establishing safety and trust.
	7. Make a video recording of a class performance a few weeks before the concert. Watch the video as a class, and lead a discussion about what is seen and heard. Continue working on the song, addressing performance issues that you and/or the students identified in the video.
	Present
	8. Present a collection of traditional songs in a public concert for families and the community. Students should use expressive singing with contrasting dynamics and tempos. Also discuss and practice performance etiquette such as stage presence, focus, etc.	

Performance Assessment	The school concert *is* the performance assessment of this task. Other assessment possibilities include student involvement in classroom discussion and personal singing development.	

	Performing Strand - First Grade	
Grade/Class	First Grade	
Date	Full Year	
<u>Primary Elemental Objective</u>	**Rhythm**: Identify, read, and perform rhythms including quarter notes, eighth notes, and quarter rests using a variety of media. Continue working to maintain steady beat.	
Secondary Elemental Objectives	**Melody**: Identify the specific pitches *la*, *so*, and *mi*, both vocally and instrumentally. Continue working to match pitch vocally. **Expression**: Explore dynamics; label, identify, and perform *piano* and *forte*. **Style**: Perform traditional children's songs and games and folk materials.	
National/State Standards	**Core Music Standards:** MU:Pr4.1.1 *With limited guidance, demonstrate and discuss personal interest in, knowledge about, and purpose of varied musical selections.* MU:Pr4.2.1 a. *With limited guidance, demonstrate knowledge of music concepts (such as beat and melodic contour) in music from a variety of cultures selected for performance.* b. *When analyzing selected music, read and perform rhythmic patterns using iconic or standard notation.* MU:Pr4.3.1 *Demonstrate and describe music's expressive qualities (such as dynamics and tempo).* MU:Pr5.1.1 a. *With limited guidance, apply personal, teacher, and peer feedback to refine performances.* b. *With limited guidance, use suggested strategies in rehearsal to address interpretive challenges of music.* MU:Pr6.1.1 a. *With limited guidance, perform music for a specific purpose with expression.* b. *Perform appropriately for the audience and purpose.*	**21st Century Skills:** • Critical Thinking & Problem Solving • Communication & Collaboration • Flexibility & Adaptability • Initiative & Self-Direction • Productivity & Accountability • Leadership & Responsibility
<u>Repertoire</u>	Current existing curricular repertoire.	
Media	Singing & Speech Barred Percussion	Unpitched and Body Percussion Movement

Performing Strand - First Grade

Process **- Experience** **- Analyze** **- Create**	*Prior Knowledge & Skills* • Maintain and identify the steady beat. • Find upper register singing voice and match pitch with a vocal model. • Demonstrate proper mallet hold and playing technique for barred percussion. *Analyze* 1. Review the concept of steady beat by performing the beat to accompany songs. Identify the difference between *beat* and *rhythm* by comparing word rhythms in songs to the beat. Introduce symbols and labels for quarter notes, two eighth notes, and quarter rest. (The author's preference is to use these real note-names from the very beginning when labeling and identifying, and to use familiar words to speak rhythms such as *blue, blue, yel-low, blue*. However, any system of syllables can work, if used consistently.) Sight-read familiar and new songs or patterns using these three rhythmic units. Perform rhythms using body percussion, unpitched percussion, barred percussion, chanting, and singing. 2. Introduce the concept of the *scale*, possibly by teaching the song "Do-Re-Mi" from *The Sound of Music*. Isolate two (*so-mi*) or three (*la-so-mi* or *mi-re-do*) pitches to explore with simple songs and games. Over the course of the year, teach and lead the class to perform a variety of traditional and/or composed songs, vocally and on barred percussion, using one of these pitch sets. Introduce staff notation, and ask students to identify rising, falling, and repeated melodic patterns. *Interpret* 3. While performing music in class, discuss expressive qualities in the music. Identify the terms *piano* and *forte*, and apply to performance based on the expressive intent of the piece. Lead a short class discussion to allow students to describe their own personal interpretation of the music. *Select* 4. After a wide variety of traditional songs have been introduced and sung in class, lead a class discussion on favorite songs. This could occur before the school concert, allowing the students to give input on which songs should be performed. The discussion should include reasons to select particular pieces, such as thematic content or performance possibilities. 5. Use a "vote" system, with multiple buckets with the name of a song on each one. Give students 1-4 sticks to place in the buckets. Tally the results in that class and across the grade, and share the results with the students. *Rehearse, Evaluate, and Refine* 6. Continue working with the class and individuals on vocal technique, such as matching pitch, breath support, and projection. Provide students with constructive feedback on barred percussion technique as well. 7. Use video or audio recording to allow students to self-assess their personal and group performances. Teach students how to give positive and constructive feedback to their peers for small group performances. *Present* 8. Present a public concert using instruments and singing, during which students demonstrate expression, good technique, and performance etiquette.
Performance Assessment	The school concert *is* the performance assessment of this task. Other assessment possibilities include student involvement in classroom discussion and personal singing and instrumental development.

Beginning in Second Grade, it will be possible for students to read and respond to simple worksheets. Whenever possible, give students a chance to demonstrate knowledge without being hindered by writing skills. For example, circling an answer is easier for a young student than writing out the words. While writing skills are important across the school curriculum, taking large amounts of time to help young students struggle through a worksheet is not beneficial to their music education.

If it is prepared properly, however, a worksheet *can* save time compared to in-class assessment of each child. For example, rather than asking each child about their favorite performance piece from the year, a worksheet allows the teacher to gather this same information from the entire class at the same time. This also ensures that the teacher does not overlook quiet students, who may not routinely participate in classroom discussions.

	Performing Strand - Second Grade	
Grade/Class	Second Grade	
Date	Full Year	
Primary Elemental Objective	**Rhythm**: Identify, read, and perform rhythms including half notes, half rests, whole notes, and whole rests using a variety of media. Identify, read, and perform 2/4 and 4/4 meters. Identify and perform an ostinato. **Melody**: Identify, read, and perform melodies including the entire *do* Pentatonic scale.	
Secondary Elemental Objectives	**Harmony**: Identify and perform a simple drone accompaniment. **Expression**: Explore dynamics; label, identify, and perform *mezzo piano* and *mezzo forte*. Explore and identify tempo markings such as *Andante*, *Allegro*, and *Largo*. **Style**: Perform a variety of traditional and modern pieces, and learn how to select and discuss preferences for specific pieces.	

National/State Standards	**Core Music Standards:**
	MU:Pr4.1.2
	    Demonstrate and explain personal interest in, knowledge about, and purpose of varied musical selections.
	MU:Pr4.2.2
	a. Demonstrate knowledge of music concepts (such as tonality and meter) in music from a variety of cultures selected for performance.
	b. When analyzing selected music, read and perform rhythmic and melodic patterns using iconic or standard notation.
	MU:Pr4.3.2
	    Demonstrate understanding of expressive qualities (such as dynamics and tempo) and how creators use them to convey expressive intent.
	MU:Pr5.1.2
	a. Apply established criteria to judge the accuracy, expressiveness, and effectiveness of performances.
	b. Rehearse, identify and apply strategies to address interpretive, performance, and technical challenges of music.
	MU:Pr6.1.2
	a. Perform music for a specific purpose with expression and technical accuracy.
	b. Perform appropriately for the audience and purpose.
		21st Century Skills:
		• Critical Thinking & Problem Solving
		• Communication & Collaboration
		• Flexibility & Adaptability
		• Initiative & Self-Direction
		• Productivity & Accountability
		• Leadership & Responsibility

Repertoire	Current existing curricular repertoire.	
Media	Singing & Speech Barred Percussion	Unpitched and Body Percussion Movement

	Performing Strand - **Second Grade**
Process **- Experience** **- Analyze** **- Create**	<u>Prior Knowledge & Skills</u> • Read and perform rhythms using quarter notes, quarter rests, and eighth notes. • Read and perform melodies using a three-pitch set such as *la-so-mi*. • Identify and perform with *piano* and *forte* dynamics. <u>Analyze</u> 1. Present a variety of repertoire that includes world folk music. While reading and analyzing the music, introduce rhythmic concepts of half notes, half rests, whole notes, whole rests, meter, time signature, and ostinato to the students. Introduce the complete Pentatonic scale for melodic study. Identify and perform simple drone accompaniments to songs. By the end of the year, students should be able to sight-read and perform using these concepts to demonstrate understanding. <u>Interpret</u> 2. While performing music in class, discuss expressive qualities in the music. Identify the terms *mezzo piano* and *mezzo forte*, and apply to performance based on the expressive intent of the piece. Identify traditional Italian tempo markings, such as *Largo*, *Andante*, and *Allegro*, and perform music at each tempo. Lead short discussions to allow students to describe their own personal interpretation of each piece of music. <u>Select</u> 3. After a wide variety of traditional songs have been introduced and sung in class, give students a repertoire voting worksheet. On the worksheet, ask each student to rank the pieces in order of preference, and then write a sentence or two describing his/her first choice (see the included worksheet). <u>Rehearse, Evaluate, and Refine</u> 4. Continue working with the class and individuals on vocal and instrumental technique as it arises in the more advanced repertoire of Second Grade. 5. During rehearsal of performance music, stop frequently to ask guiding questions about performance aspects such as balance, tempo, and dynamics. 6. Create reflection sheets for students to fill out when observing video or audio recordings of their own performances (see the included reflection sheet) <u>Present</u> 7. Present a public concert using instruments and singing, during which students demonstrate expression, good technique, and performance etiquette.
Performance Assessment	Concert performance videos, class discussions, and worksheets provide ample documentation of assessment.

Song Selection Sheet

Second Grade

Name: _____   Date: _____

Class: _____

Below are listed most of the songs that we have learned so far this year. Number the songs from 1-8, with 1 being your favorite, or first choice for performance, and 8 being your last choice.

_____   _____

_____   _____

_____   _____

_____   _____

Next, describe your first choice (#1) by circling the best description word in each row:

happy   *sad*   *exciting*   *relaxing*

Allegro (fast)   *Andante (medium)*   *Largo (slow)*

In your own words, describe the meaning of the song that you chose as #1:

_____
_____
_____
_____

Performance Reflection Sheet

Second Grade

Name: _____   Date: _____

Class: _____

Write the name of the music being performed: _____

Were you one of the performers?   yes   no

Singing was: *mostly on pitch*   *not on pitch*

Could you understand the words of the song?   yes   no

Did individual parts, such as ostinati, stay together with the group?   yes   no

Could you hear a good balance of singing and instruments?   yes   no

What was the dynamic (volume) level of the performance?

piano   *mezzo piano*   *mezzo forte*   *forte*

What was the tempo (speed) of the performance?

    Largo (slow)   *Andante (medium)*   *Allegro (fast)*

What suggestions would you have to improve the performance?

_____
_____
_____
_____

	Performing Strand - Third Grade	
Grade/Class	Third Grade	
Date	Full Year	
Primary Elemental Objective	**Rhythm**: Identify, read, and perform rhythms in 3/4 time, including dotted half notes and eighth/quarter/eighth syncopation. **Melody**: Identify, read, *transpose*, and perform melodies including expanded *do* Pentatonic (high *do*, low *la* and *so*), *la* Pentatonic, *re* Pentatonic, and *so* Pentatonic.	
Secondary Elemental Objectives	**Harmony**: Identify and perform shifting harmonies such as a moving drone. Identify and perform a 2-part or 3-part round. **Expression**: Explore dynamics; label, identify, and perform *pianissimo* and *fortissimo*. **Style**: Perform a variety of traditional and modern pieces, and learn how to select and discuss preferences for specific pieces.	

National/State Standards	**Core Music Standards:**
	MU:Pr4.1.3
	    Demonstrate and explain how the selection of music to perform is influenced by personal interest, knowledge, purpose, and context.
	MU:Pr4.2.3
	a. Demonstrate understanding of the structure in music selected for performance.
	b. When analyzing selected music, read and perform rhythmic patterns and melodic phrases using iconic and standard notation.
	c. Describe how context (such as personal and social) can inform a performance.
	MU:Pr4.3.3
	    Demonstrate and describe how intent is conveyed through expressive qualities (such as dynamics and tempo).
	MU:Pr5.1.3
	a. Apply teacher-provided and collaboratively-developed criteria and feedback to evaluate accuracy of ensemble performances.
	b. Rehearse to refine technical accuracy, expressive qualities, and identified performance challenges.
	MU:Pr6.1.3
	a. Perform music with expression and technical accuracy.
	b. Demonstrate performance decorum and audience etiquette appropriate for the context and venue.
		21st Century Skills:
		• Critical Thinking & Problem Solving
		• Communication & Collaboration
		• Flexibility & Adaptability
		• Initiative & Self-Direction
		• Productivity & Accountability
		• Leadership & Responsibility

Repertoire	Current existing curricular repertoire.	
Media	Singing & Speech Barred Percussion	Unpitched and Body Percussion Movement

	Performing Strand - Third Grade
Process **- Experience** **- Analyze** **- Create**	*Prior Knowledge & Skills* • Read and perform rhythms using quarter notes, quarter rests, eighth notes, half notes, half rests, whole notes, and whole rests. Identify the time signatures of 2/4 and 4/4. • Read and perform melodies using the *do* Pentatonic scale. • Identify and perform with varied dynamics (*p, mp, mf, f*) and tempos. *Analyze* 1. Present a variety of repertoire that includes world folk music. While reading and analyzing the music, introduce rhythmic concepts of dotted half notes, syncopation, and 3/4 time to the students. Introduce the melodic concepts of transposition and new Pentatonic modes (*la* Pentatonic, *re* Pentatonic, and *so* Pentatonic). Identify and label phrase forms (e.g., *aaba*) and sectional forms (such as verse/chorus and rondo) in performance repertoire. Identify and perform a round in two or more parts. Identify and perform a shifting harmony part such as a moving drone. By the end of the year, students should be able to sight-read and perform, using these concepts to demonstrate understanding. 2. Lead a classroom discussion, including various live and recorded performance examples, about why certain music is chosen for specific events, such as holidays and parades. *Interpret* 3. While performing music in class, discuss expressive qualities in the music. Identify the terms *pianissimo* and *fortissimo*. Continue exploring a variety of tempos and dynamics. Lead short discussions to allow students to describe their own personal interpretation of each piece of music. *Select* 4. After a wide variety of traditional and composed songs have been introduced and sung in class, give students a repertoire voting worksheet. On the worksheet, ask each student to rank the pieces in order of preference, and then write a sentence or two about why he/she selected his/her first choice (see the included worksheet). *Rehearse, Evaluate, and Refine* 5. Continue working with the class and individuals on vocal and instrumental technique as it arises in the repertoire. Sing and/or play parts in harmony, such as a two-part round or melodic ostinato accompanying a melody. 6. During rehearsal of performance music, stop frequently to ask guiding questions about performance aspects such as balance, tempo, and dynamics. 7. Create reflection sheets for students to fill out when observing video or audio recordings of their own performances (see the included reflection sheet). *Present* 8. Present a public concert using instruments and singing, during which students demonstrate expression, good technique, and performance etiquette.
Performance Assessment	Concert performance videos, class discussions, and worksheets provide ample documentation of assessment.

Song Selection Sheet

Third Grade

Name: _____   Date: _____

Class: _____

Below are listed most of the songs that we have learned so far this year. Number the songs from 1-8, with 1 being your favorite, or first choice for performance, and 8 being your last choice.

_____   _____

_____   _____

_____   _____

_____   _____

In your own words, describe the meaning of the song that you chose as #1.

_____
_____
_____
_____

What was your personal reason for choosing this song?

_____
_____
_____
_____

Performance Reflection Sheet

Third Grade

Name: _____   Date: _____

Class: _____

Write the name of the music being performed: _____

Were you one of the performers?   yes   no

Singing was: *mostly on pitch*   *not on pitch*

Could you understand the words of the song?   yes   no

Did individual parts such, as ostinati, stay together with the group?   yes   no

Could you hear a good balance of singing and instruments?   yes   no

What was the dynamic (volume) level of the performance?

pianissimo   piano   mezzo-piano   mezzo-forte   forte   fortissimo

What was the tempo (speed) of the performance?

Largo (slow)   Andante (medium)   Allegro (fast)

What suggestions would you have to improve the performance?

_____
_____
_____
_____

Beginning in Fourth Grade, we will allow students not only to give input on their favorite songs from class, but also to suggest and present their own ideas for future performance. Depending on your students and schedule, this can either be incredibly productive *or* frustratingly time-consuming. Decide ahead of time whether this work will be done in class or as homework. If done in class, you must make arrangements to give students access to the internet for research. This can be done all at once, such as by reserving a computer lab, or a few students can work at a time on a computer in the back of the music room. It is also possible to do "stations," and have multiple class activities happen simultaneously. For example, while some students research their music proposal, others can practice an instrument quietly, compose, or choreograph a dance. Create a rotation schedule so that all students get the benefit of each of these stations, making sure that each activity is fairly self-explanatory.

If assigned as homework, you need to be prepared with an alternate plan for those students who cannot or do not complete the assignment within a reasonable amount of time. This could be the same as the in-class ideas above, but only for those students who do not complete the assignment at home.

Be sure to discuss appropriate and inappropriate content ahead of time, and then pre-screen all examples. If students complain that the only music to which they listen is inappropriate, challenge them to find new music and expand their experience. Having a partner to work with could help students find more variety of musical selections.

Notice also that the upper elementary grade worksheets require more writing. Be prepared to accommodate students who have IEP or other plans for writing. Some students need a scribe, while others simply need extra time. Once again, working with a partner might enable a student with special needs to successfully complete the assignment.

	Performing Strand - Fourth Grade	
Grade/Class	Fourth Grade	
Date	Full Year	
Primary Elemental Objective	**Rhythm**: Identify, read, and perform rhythms including sixteenth notes. **Melody**: Identify, read, and perform melodies using the Hexatonic, major, and minor scales.	
Secondary Elemental Objectives	**Harmony**: Sing and play partner songs and simple homophonic harmonies. **Expression**: Identify, label, and perform *crescendo*, *decrescendo/diminuendo*, *ritardando*, and *accelerando*. **Style**: Select a particular piece of music, describe it, and explain why it should be performed by the class.	

National/State Standards	**Core Music Standards:**
	MU:Pr4.1.4
	    Demonstrate and explain how the selection of music to perform is influenced by personal interest, knowledge, context, and technical skill.
	MU:Pr4.2.4
	a. *Demonstrate understanding of the structure and the elements of music (such as rhythm, pitch, and form) in music selected for performance.*
	b. *When analyzing selected music, read and perform using iconic and/or standard notation.*
	c. *Explain how context (such as social and cultural) informs a performance.*
	MU:Pr4.3.4
	    Demonstrate and explain how intent is conveyed through interpretive decisions and expressive qualities (such as dynamics, tempo, and timbre).
	MU:Pr5.1.4
	a. *Apply teacher-provided and collaboratively-developed criteria and feedback to evaluate accuracy and expressiveness of ensemble and personal performances.*
	b. *Rehearse to refine technical accuracy and expressive qualities, and address performance challenges.*
	MU:Pr6.1.4
	a. *Perform music, alone or with others, with expression and technical accuracy, and appropriate interpretation.*
	b. *Demonstrate performance decorum and audience etiquette appropriate for the context, venue, and genre.*
		21st Century Skills:
		• Creativity & Innovation
		• Critical Thinking & Problem Solving
		• Communication & Collaboration
		• Flexibility & Adaptability
		• Initiative & Self-Direction
		• Productivity & Accountability
		• Leadership & Responsibility

Repertoire	Current existing curricular repertoire.	

	Performing Strand - **Fourth Grade**	
Media	Singing & Speech Barred Percussion & Recorder	Unpitched and Body Percussion Movement
Process **- Experience** **- Analyze** **- Create**	<p>*Prior Knowledge & Skills*</p><ul><li>Read and perform rhythms using quarter notes, quarter rests, eighth notes, half notes, half rests, whole notes, whole rests, dotted rhythms, and syncopation. Identify time signatures of 2/4, 4/4, and 3/4.</li><li>Read and perform melodies using the *do* and *la* Pentatonic scales in multiple keys (F-*do*, G-*do*, C-*do*, A-*la*, D-*la*, E-*la*).</li><li>Identify and perform with varied dynamics (*pp-ff*) and tempos.</li></ul><p>*Analyze*</p><ol><li>Present a variety of repertoire that includes world folk music and some historical music (e.g., Western Art music). While reading and analyzing the music, introduce the rhythmic concept of sixteenth notes to the students. Introduce reading and analysis of Hexatonic, major, and minor scales, using *fa* and *ti*. Identify longer sectional forms and advanced harmonies (such as partner songs and homophonic harmony) used in performance. By the end of the year, students should be able to sight-read and perform using these concepts to demonstrate understanding.</li><li>Lead a classroom discussion, including various live and recorded performance examples, of why certain music is chosen for specific events, like holidays, parades, weddings, and concerts or for specific purposes, such as movies and commercials.</li></ol><p>*Interpret*</p><ol start="3"><li>While performing music in class, discuss expressive qualities in the music. Identify the terms *crescendo, decrescendo/diminuendo, ritardando*, and *accelerando*. Continue exploring a variety of tempos and dynamics. Lead short discussions to allow students to describe their own personal interpretation of each piece of music.</li></ol><p>*Select*</p><ol start="4"><li>After a wide variety of songs have been introduced and sung in class, give students a repertoire voting worksheet. On the worksheet, ask each student to rank the pieces in order of preference, and then write a sentence or two about why he/she selected his/her first choice.</li><li>Give students a separate worksheet on which to suggest a new piece of music (such as popular music) that they would enjoy singing in class. Students should describe the piece—what it is about, why it should be sung in class, and what arranging would be necessary for the class to perform it (see the included worksheet).</li><li>Once students have filled out the worksheets, compile the song suggestions from the class, and select one popular song to add to the class repertoire. Discuss in class how you selected the piece based on the proposals.</li></ol><p>*Rehearse, Evaluate, and Refine*</p><ol start="7"><li>Continue working with the class and individuals on vocal and instrumental technique as it arises in the repertoire.</li><li>During rehearsal of performance music, stop frequently to ask guiding questions about performance aspects such as balance, tempo, and dynamics.</li><li>Create reflection sheets for students to fill out when observing video or audio recordings of their own performances (see the included reflection sheet).</li></ol><p>*Present*</p><ol start="10"><li>Present a public concert using instruments and singing, during which students demonstrate expression, good technique, and performance etiquette.</li></ol>	
Performance Assessment	Concert performance videos, class discussions, and worksheets provide ample documentation of assessment.	

Song Selection Sheet

Fourth Grade

Name: _____   Date: _____

Class: _____

Below are listed most of the songs that we have learned so far this year. Number the songs from 1-8, with 1 being your favorite, or first choice for performance, and 8 being your last choice.

_____   _____

_____   _____

_____   _____

_____   _____

In your own words, describe the meaning of the song that you chose as #1.

_____
_____
_____
_____

What was your personal reason for choosing this song?

_____
_____
_____
_____

Song Proposal Sheet

Fourth Grade

Name: _____   Date: _____

Class: _____

Write down the title of a piece of music that *you* would like the class to perform. Keep in mind that songs with explicit lyrics will *not* be chosen.

_____

Who is the performer or composer of this piece?

_____

In what year did this piece come out?

_____

What is the style of this piece of music? How do you know?

_____
_____
_____

What is the meaning of the song/lyrics? What is it about?

_____
_____
_____
_____

(worksheet continued on next page)

(4th Grade Song Proposal Sheet p. 2)

What are your suggestions for how we could perform this song with the class (instruments, voice parts, arrangement)?

_____
_____
_____
_____

Why did you select this piece? What does it mean to you?

_____
_____
_____
_____

Performance Reflection Sheet

Fourth Grade

Name: _____   Date: _____

Class: _____

Write the name of the music being performed: _____

Were you one of the performers?   *yes*   *no*

Singing was: *mostly on pitch*   *not on pitch*

Could you understand the words of the song?   *yes*   *no*

Did individual parts stay together with the group?   *yes*   *no*

Could you hear a good balance of singing and instruments?   *yes*   *no*

What was the dynamic (volume) level of the performance?

pianissimo   *piano*   *mezzo-piano*   *mezzo-forte*   *forte*   *fortissimo*

What was the tempo (speed) of the performance?

Largo (slow)   *Andante (medium)*   *Allegro (fast)*

What suggestions would you have to improve the performance?

_____
_____
_____
_____

	Performing Strand - Fifth Grade
Grade/Class	Fifth Grade
Date	Full Year
Primary Elemental Objective	**Rhythm**: Identify, read, and perform rhythms in compound meters, such as 6/8. **Melody**: Identify, read, and perform melodies using the Dorian, Phrygian, Lydian, and Mixolydian modes.
Secondary Elemental Objectives	**Harmony**: Identify and perform chord progressions. **Style**: Select a particular piece of music, describe it, and explain why it should be performed by the class.

National/State Standards	**Core Music Standards:**
	MU:Pr4.1.5
	    Demonstrate and explain how the selection of music to perform is influenced by personal interest, knowledge, and context, as well as their personal and others' technical skill.
	MU:Pr4.2.5
	a. Demonstrate understanding of the structure and the elements of music (such as rhythm, pitch, form, and harmony) in music selected for performance.
	b. When analyzing selected music, read and perform using standard notation.
	c. Explain how context (such as social, cultural, and historical) informs performances.
	MU:Pr4.3.5
	    Demonstrate and explain how intent is conveyed through interpretive decisions and expressive qualities (such as dynamics, tempo, timbre, and articulation/style).
	MU:Pr5.1.5
	a. Apply teacher-provided and established criteria and feedback to evaluate the accuracy and expressiveness of ensemble and personal performances.
	b. Rehearse to refine technical accuracy and expressive qualities to address challenges, and show improvement over time.
	MU:Pr6.1.5
	a. Perform music, alone or with others, with expression, technical accuracy, and appropriate interpretation.
	b. Demonstrate performance decorum and audience etiquette appropriate for the context, venue, genre, and style.
		21st Century Skills:
		• Creativity & Innovation
		• Critical Thinking & Problem Solving
		• Communication & Collaboration
		• Flexibility & Adaptability
		• Initiative & Self-Direction
		• Productivity & Accountability
		• Leadership & Responsibility

Repertoire	Current existing curricular repertoire.

	Performing Strand - Fifth Grade	
Media	Singing & Speech Barred Percussion & Recorder	Unpitched and Body Percussion Movement
Process **- Experience** **- Analyze** **- Create**	*Prior Knowledge & Skills* • Read and perform traditional rhythms in various simple meters. • Read and perform melodies using the major and minor scales in various keys. • Identify and perform with varied dynamics and tempos. *Analyze* 1. Present a variety of repertoire that includes world folk music, historical music, and popular music. While reading and analyzing the music, introduce reading and analysis of compound time. Introduce scale modes such as Dorian, Phrygian, Lydian, and Mixolydian. Introduce functional harmonies including I-IV-V chords. By the end of the year, students should be able to sight-read and perform using these concepts to demonstrate understanding. 2. Lead a classroom discussion, including various live and recorded performance examples, of why certain music is chosen for specific events, like holidays, parades, weddings, and concerts or for specific purposes, such as movies and commercials. *Interpret* 3. As part of the selection process below, ask students to describe the composer's intent in writing a piece of music. *Select* 4. After a wide variety of songs have been introduced and sung in class, give students a repertoire voting worksheet. On the worksheet, ask each student to rank the pieces in order of preference, and then write a sentence or two about why he/she selected his/her first choice. 5. Assign students to research a piece of popular music, and then fill out a worksheet describing why they feel the class should perform that piece. 6. Once students have filled out the worksheets, compile the song suggestions from the class, and select one or more popular songs to add to the class repertoire. Discuss in class how you selected the piece or pieces based on the proposals. Alternatively, you could lead a group discussion, and let the class vote on a final selection. *Rehearse, Evaluate, and Refine* 7. Continue working with the class and individuals on vocal and instrumental technique as it arises in the repertoire. 8. During rehearsal of performance music, stop frequently to ask guiding questions about performance aspects such as balance, tempo, and dynamics. 9. Create reflection sheets for students to fill out when observing video or audio recordings of their own performances. *Present* 10. Present a public concert using instruments and singing, during which students demonstrate expression, good technique, and performance etiquette.	
Performance Assessment	Concert performance videos, class discussions, and worksheets provide ample documentation of assessment.	

Song Selection Sheet

Fifth Grade

Name: _____   Date: _____

Class: _____

Below are listed many of the songs that we have learned so far this year. Number the songs from 1-8, with 1 being your favorite, or first choice for performance, and 8 being your last choice.

_____   _____

_____   _____

_____   _____

_____   _____

In your own words, describe the meaning of the song that you chose as #1. What was the composer's intent in writing the music?

_____
_____
_____
_____

What was your personal reason for choosing this song?

_____
_____
_____
_____

Song Proposal Sheet

Fifth Grade

Name: _____   Date: _____

Class: _____

Write down the title of a piece of music that *you* would like the class to perform. Keep in mind that songs with explicit lyrics will *not* be chosen.

_____

Who is the performer or composer of this piece?

_____

In what year did this piece come out?

_____

What is the style of this piece of music? How do you know?

_____

_____

_____

What is the meaning of the song/lyrics? What is it about?

_____

_____

_____

_____

(worksheet continued on next page)

(4th Grade Song Proposal Sheet p. 2)

What are your suggestions for how we could perform this song with the class (instruments, voice parts, arrangement)?

_____
_____
_____
_____

Why did you select this piece? What does it mean to you? Why is it a good suggestion for the class?

_____
_____
_____
_____

Performance Reflection Sheet
Fifth Grade

Name: _____   Date: _____

Class: _____

Write the name of the music being performed: _____

Singing was: *mostly on pitch*   *not on pitch*

Could you understand the words of the song?   *yes*   *no*

Did individual parts stay together with the group?   *yes*   *no*

Could you hear a good balance of singing and instruments?   *yes*   *no*

What was the dynamic (volume) level of the performance?

pianissimo   *piano*   *mezzo-piano*   *mezzo-forte*   *forte*   *fortissimo*

What was the tempo (speed) of the performance?

Largo (slow)   *Andante (medium)*   *Allegro (fast)*

What mode was the song written in?

Ionian(major)   *Dorian*   *Phrygian*   *Mixolydian*   *Lydian*   *Aeolian(minor)*

What suggestions would you have to improve the performance?

_____
_____
_____
_____

Artistic Process: Responding

As with the Performance process, the Responding Process is written with a focus on analyzing, selecting, and interpreting. While discussion and written reflection make perfect sense when listening to music, you must still take care to not allow these activities to limit active music making. In a creative classroom, listening examples should directly connect to the performance pieces and compositional techniques being applied. For example, students can listen to *and* perform works from a particular style or culture, and then use those examples as inspiration to craft their own original works.

Since the quantity and variety of recorded music in the 21st century is so vast, teachers by necessity must pick and choose what is to be presented in class. It is helpful to sequence a list of works based on style, but aligned with performance and creative learning. Below is a short list of possibilities, based on this author's preferences. Be sure to select those pieces that you personally have enjoyed, as your own enthusiasm for the music can inspire your students to learn more about a style or genre.

Listening Examples					
Kindergarten	**First**	**Second**	**Third**	**Fourth**	**Fifth**
March: "Stars & Stripes Forever" (steady beat)	**Ballet**: *The Nutcracker*	**Tone Poem/ Orchestral Suite**: *Peer Gynt*	**Opera**: *William Tell* ("Overture"), *Hansel & Gretel*	**Jazz**: "Duke's Place"	**Orchestral Suite**: *The Planets*
Orchestral Suite: *Carnival of the Animals* (melodic line)	**Narrated Story**: *Peter & the Wolf* (solo instruments)	**Symphony**: #94 by Haydn	**Tone Poem**: *Danse Macabre*, "Flight of the Bumblebee"	**Symphony**: #4 by Tchaikovsky #5 by Beethoven	**Symphony**: #9 by Beethoven
	Dance: "Carnivalito" (ostinato)	**Choral Work**: *Carmina Burana*		**Opera**: *The Magic Flute*	**Musical**: *The Sound of Music*
	Piano: "Ah Vous Dirai-je" (variations)				**Jazz**: "Take Five" (5/4 time)
	Percussion Ensemble: "Street Song"				

Although the lessons here refer to recorded examples for simplicity, remember also that *listening* and *responding* can refer as well to live performances, such as guest performers, teacher modeling, and peer performances.

	Responding Strand - Kindergarten	
Grade/Class	Kindergarten	
Date	Full Year	
<u>**Primary Elemental Objective**</u>	**Rhythm**: Identify and follow the steady beat while listening to music. Use body percussion or unpitched percussion to play with the beat.	
Secondary Elemental Objectives	**Melody**: Identify high, low, and melodic direction while listening to music. Use movement and/or line drawing to demonstrate awareness of melodic direction. **Style**: Listen to music of a variety of styles.	

National/State Standards	**Core Music Standards:**
	MU:Re7.1.K
	    With guidance, list personal interests and experiences and demonstrate why they prefer some music selections over others.
	MU:Re7.2.K
	    With guidance, demonstrate how a specific music concept (such as beat or melodic direction) is used in music.
	MU:Re8.1.K
	    With guidance, demonstrate awareness of expressive qualities (such as dynamics and tempo) that reflect creators'/performers' expressive intent.
	MU:Re9.1.K
	    With guidance, apply personal and expressive preferences in the evaluation of music.
		21st Century Skills:
		• Creativity & Innovation
		• Critical Thinking & Problem Solving
		• Communication & Collaboration
		• Flexibility & Adaptability
		• Initiative & Self-Direction
		• Productivity & Accountability
		• Leadership & Responsibility

<u>**Repertoire**</u>	*Carnival of the Animals* by C. Saint-Saëns "Stars and Stripes Forever" by J.P. Sousa	
<u>**Media**</u>	Movement Body Percussion	Unpitched Percussion

Responding Strand - Kindergarten

Process
- Experience
- Analyze
- Create
	Prior Knowledge & Skills
	• Be able to sit or move silently while listening to music.
	Analyze
	1. Play a variety of recordings of high quality music for the class.
	2. As the class listens to music with a clear melodic line, have them demonstrate understanding of the rising and falling pitch by one of the following activities. This can be thematically connected to the piece of music. For example, when listening to "Aquarium" from Saint-Saëns *Carnival of the Animals*, students can draw or act out the movement of a fish.
	   a. move hand up and down to the music
	   b. move a prop such as a scarf or ribbon
	   c. move entire body (dance)
	   d. draw a line on a piece of paper to show the rising and falling
	3. When listening to music with a clear sense of pulse, have the class demonstrate their feeling of beat with one of the following, which again could be thematic, such as pretending to march in a band while listening to "Stars and Stripes Forever" by Sousa.
	   a. march or step to the beat
	   b. clap or pat the beat
	   c. play a drum or other percussion instrument with the beat
	Interpret
	4. While listening to and exploring various recordings, lead the class in responding to dynamics (loud/soft) and tempo (fast/slow) through changes in creatively-themed movement or playing of the steady beat.
	Select
	5. After listening and responding to several contrasting musical selections, ask the class to identify and discuss their favorite recording. For example, if listening to multiple movements from *Carnival of the Animals*, students could be asked to stand in groups based on their preferences for individual movements. Within each group, students can then describe why they prefer that movement and share these ideas with the whole class.
	Evaluate
	6. Continuing the discussion about personal preference, play two contrasting recordings of the *same* piece of music. Ask students to describe why they prefer one version over the other.

Performance Assessment	Assess melodic contour, beat awareness, and expressive change through movement responses.

	Responding Strand - First Grade	
Grade/Class	First Grade	
Date	Full Year	
Primary Elemental Objective	**Rhythm**: Identify and follow repeated rhythmic patterns while listening to music. Use movement, body percussion, or unpitched percussion to play along with the rhythm patterns.	
Secondary Elemental Objectives	**Melody**: Identify high, low, and melodic contour while listening to music. Use movement and/or line drawing to demonstrate awareness of melodic contours. **Style**: Listen to music of a variety of styles. Identify specific instruments and voice types.	
National/State Standards	**Core Music Standards:** *MU:Re7.1.1* *With limited guidance, identify and demonstrate how personal interests and experiences influence musical selection for specific purposes.* *MU:Re7.2.1* *With limited guidance, demonstrate and identify how specific music concepts (such as beat or pitch) are used in various styles of music for a purpose.* *MU:Re8.1.1* *With limited guidance, demonstrate and identify expressive qualities (such as dynamics and tempo) that reflect creators'/performers' expressive intent.* *MU:Re9.1.1* *With limited guidance, apply personal and expressive preferences in the evaluation of music for specific purposes.*	**21st Century Skills:** • Creativity & Innovation • Critical Thinking & Problem Solving • Communication & Collaboration • Flexibility & Adaptability • Initiative & Self-Direction • Productivity & Accountability • Leadership & Responsibility
Repertoire	"Carnivalito" by Shenanigans "12 Variations on 'Ah Vous Dirai-je, Maman'" by W.A. Mozart "Street Song (Gassenhäuer)" by Carl Orff / Gunild Keetman *Peter and the Wolf* by Prokofiev	
Media	Singing Movement	Body Percussion Unpitched Percussion

Responding Strand - First Grade

Process **- Experience** **- Analyze** **- Create**	*Prior Knowledge & Skills* • Maintain a steady beat while listening to recorded music. • Demonstrate high/low, loud/soft, and fast/slow in response to recorded music. *Analyze* 1. Continue to play a variety of recordings of high-quality music for the class. Choose specific styles, cultures, ensembles, or time periods, and connect these choices with the rest of your curriculum. 2. As the class listens to music with a clear melodic line, have them continue to demonstrate understanding of the rising and falling pitch. Choose a piece with a clear, specific melodic line, and show the students the notation (or graphic notation) for this theme. Ask them to trace the shape of the melodic line with hands, props, or a writing tool. An example would be "12 Variations on 'Ah Vous Dirai-je, Maman'" (Twinkle) by Mozart. Listen and respond in connection with lessons teaching this melody vocally. Connect this listening activity with singing familiar lyrics to the tune. 3. When listening to music with a clear sense of pulse, have the class continue to demonstrate the steady beat. Select one or more recordings which demonstrate a clear, repeated rhythmic pattern, such as "Street Song (Gassenhäuer)" by Carl Orff and Gunild Keetman (*Music for Children Vol. IV*). Identify the repeated rhythmic pattern, and ask the class to clap or play a percussion instrument along with the pattern. Use graphic or standard rhythmic notation to reinforce the concept. "Street Song" actually layers several simple rhythmic ostinati, each of which can be studied and performed with the recording. 4. Find a folk dance recording, such as "Carnivalito" by Shenanigans, and lead the class in stepping to the rhythm of the music. By moving with the music, the students experience the traditional dance *and* demonstrate awareness of rhythm in listening. *Interpret* 5. While listening to and exploring various recordings, have the class demonstrate awareness of dynamics (loud/soft) and tempo (fast/slow) through changes in creatively-themed movement or playing of the steady beat. Students should be able to identify and demonstrate changes with little teacher direction. For example, in the "12 Variations," students could create distinct motions for each variation, and help the teacher use graphic notation or words to describe each individual variation. 6. Play a recording of *Peter and the Wolf* by Prokofiev for the students. Use visuals of the various instruments. Discuss why the composer chose specific instruments to represent specific characters in the story, and how the composer used dynamics or tempo to affect the mood of the piece. *Select* 7. After listening and responding to several contrasting musical selections, ask the class to identify and discuss their favorite recording. Lead a class discussion, identifying the positive aspects of each recording, and take a class vote for one piece to listen to again and study further. *Evaluate* 8. Continuing the discussion about personal preference, play two contrasting recordings of the *same* piece of music. This could, for example, compare a vocal version to an instrumental version. There are many recordings of "Twinkle Twinkle," so this would be a good example. Ask students to describe why they prefer one version over the other.
Performance Assessment	Assess melodic contour, rhythmic/beat awareness, and expressive change through movement responses. Use cue cards or other visuals to assess identification of instruments.

Since many of the separate strands (analyze & interpret, select & evaluate) of the *Responding* process can be accomplished with a single discussion or worksheet, the following lessons have combined these Performance Standards in the process steps.

	Responding Strand - Second Grade	
Grade/Class	Second Grade	
Date	Full Year	
Primary Elemental Objective	**Style**: Identify and discuss specific styles of music, such as choral and orchestral. Demonstrate personal preferences for specific pieces of music.	
Secondary Elemental Objectives	**Expression**: Use drama and movement to interpret and demonstrate awareness of musical storytelling. Identify dynamics, tempos, and articulations, and incorporate these into movement/drama performance.	
National/State Standards	**Core Music Standards:** *MU:Re7.1.2* 　*Explain and demonstrate how personal interests and experiences influence musical selection for specific purposes.* *MU:Re7.2.2* 　*Describe how specific music concepts are used to support a specific purpose in music.* *MU:Re8.1.2* 　*Demonstrate knowledge of music concepts and how they support creators'/performers' expressive intent.* *MU:Re9.1.2* 　*Apply personal and expressive preferences in the evaluation of music for specific purposes.*	**21st Century Skills:** • Creativity & Innovation • Critical Thinking & Problem Solving • Communication & Collaboration • Flexibility & Adaptability • Initiative & Self-Direction • Productivity & Accountability • Leadership & Responsibility
Repertoire	"In the Hall of the Mountain King" from *Peer Gynt Suite* by Edvard Grieg "Andante" from *Symphony #94* by F.J. Haydn "O Fortuna" from *Carmina Burana* by Carl Orff	
Media	Drama	Movement

Responding Strand - Second Grade

Process **- Experience** **- Analyze** **- Create**	*Prior Knowledge & Skills* • Maintain a steady beat while listening to recorded music. • Demonstrate melodic line and repeated rhythmic patterns in response to recorded music. *Analyze & Interpret* 1. Continue to play a variety of recordings of high-quality music for the class. Choose specific styles, cultures, ensembles, or time periods, and connect these choices with the rest of your curriculum. 2. Play a selection such as the "Allegro" movement from Haydn's *Symphony #94*. Ask students to describe musical elements that Haydn uses to achieve "surprise." Discuss why a composer might choose to surprise the audience. Apply identified surprise elements to a small group or class choreography to accompany the music. 3. Play recordings in which a composer tells a story through music, such as "In the Hall of the Mountain King" from *Peer Gynt Suite* by Grieg. Use listening maps or other visuals to help students follow the story. Discuss how the composer's writing and the performers' playing feature elements of music to tell the story. Assign actors, and let the class silently act out the music while listening. 4. Discuss and review the families of instruments, such as brass, woodwind, string, and percussion. Ask students to identify when each family is heard in recordings. 5. Use responding worksheets, such as those included on the next few pages, to assess student understanding of musical elements in the recordings. *Select & Evaluate* 6. While presenting various recordings throughout the year, lead a discussion about the different events and settings that feature live music, such as parades, orchestra concerts, football games, or holiday caroling. Discuss how the setting of each performance influences the type of music performed. Using a recording such as "O Fortuna" from *Carmina Burana* by Orff, discuss how a work of music can often be repurposed for commercial use. 7. After listening and responding to several contrasting musical selections, give students a worksheet on which to select their favorite recordings. Use multiple-choice type questions to assess understanding of musical elements in the recording. Lead a discussion about favorite pieces and the reason they are favorites. 8. Continuing the discussion about personal preference, play two contrasting recordings of the *same* piece of music.
Performance Assessment	Assess understanding of expressive elements through dramatic and movement exploration and performance. Use the included worksheets to assess analysis and the ability to express personal preference for listening examples.

Listening Evaluation Sheet

Second Grade

Name: _____   Date: _____

Class: _____

Write the name of the music being performed: _____

Was the music: *vocal*   *instrumental*   *both* ?

If you heard instruments, circle the families of instruments you heard:

    strings   *woodwinds*   *brass*   *percussion*

If you heard voices, circle the types of voices you heard: *men*   *women*   *children*

What was the main tempo (speed) of the performance?

    Largo (slow)   *Andante (medium)*   *Allegro (fast)*

What was the main dynamic (volume level) of the performance?   *piano*   *forte*

What was the mood of the performance? *happy*   *sad*   *exciting*   *relaxing*

What is your favorite part of this recording?

_____

_____

What is your least favorite part?

_____

_____

Listening Selection Sheet

Second Grade

Name: _____   Date: _____

Class: _____

Below are listed most of the recorded pieces that we have listened to so far this year. Number the pieces from 1-4, with 1 being your favorite, or first choice, and 4 being your last choice.

_____   _____

_____   _____

Next, describe your first choice (#1) by circling the best description word in each row:

happy   *sad*   *exciting*   *relaxing*

Allegro (fast)   *Andante (medium)*   *Largo (slow)*

In your own words, describe what you know about your #1 choice:

_____
_____
_____
_____

	Responding Strand - Third Grade	
Grade/Class	Third Grade	
Date	Full Year	
Primary Elemental Objective	**Style**: Identify and discuss specific styles of music, such as ballet and opera. Demonstrate personal preferences for specific pieces of music. Evaluate performances for quality and content.	
Secondary Elemental Objectives	**Expression**: Use drama and movement to interpret and demonstrate awareness of musical storytelling. Identify dynamics, tempos, and articulations, and incorporate these into movement/drama performance.	
National/State Standards	**Core Music Standards:** *MU:Re7.1.3* *Demonstrate and describe how selected music connects to and is influenced by specific interests, experiences, or purposes.* *MU:Re7.2.3* *Demonstrate and describe how a response to music can be informed by the structure, the use of the elements of music, and context (such as personal and social).* *MU:Re8.1.3* *Demonstrate and describe how the expressive qualities (such as dynamics and tempo) are used in performers' interpretations to reflect expressive intent.* *MU:Re9.1.3* *Evaluate musical works and performances, applying established criteria, and describe appropriateness to the context.*	**21st Century Skills:** • Creativity & Innovation • Critical Thinking & Problem Solving • Communication & Collaboration • Flexibility & Adaptability • Initiative & Self-Direction • Productivity & Accountability • Leadership & Responsibility
Repertoire	*Danse Macabre* by C. Saint-Saëns 'Flight of the Bumblebee" by N. Rimsky-Korsakov "Overture" from *William Tell* by Rossini	
Media	Drama	Movement

Responding Strand - Third Grade

Process **- Experience** **- Analyze** **- Create**	*Prior Knowledge & Skills* • Identify rhythm and melodic line in recorded music. • Identify dynamics and tempos in recorded music. • Identify the four families of instruments and various voice types in recorded music. *Analyze & Interpret* 1. Continue to play a variety of recordings of high-quality music for the class. Choose specific styles, cultures, ensembles, or time periods, and connect these choices with the rest of your curriculum. 2. Play a selection such as the "Overture" from *William Tell* by Rossini. (The main theme begins after about seven minutes, but you can also listen from the beginning for more contrast.) Before giving the title of the work or storyline from the opera, ask the students to describe, draw, or write about a scene that they picture in their mind. Discuss how specific elements of the music, such as dynamics, tempo, instrumentation, rhythms and melodies help tell a story. Later, give students a synopsis of the actual story behind the music, and ask them if they think that the composer's music fits the story. Discuss how an overture takes all of the main themes from the story and presents them together. 3. Act out and/or dance stories set to music such as *Danse Macabre* by Saint-Saëns. While you provide the characters and overall plot, the students must decide upon the specific actions, based on the changes in the music. Discuss and show examples of how ballet choreographers follow this same process. 4. Review the families of instruments, and identify specific instruments for study and listening. Choose music that features solo instruments, such as the violin in *Danse Macabre*. 5. Use worksheets, such as those included, to assess student understanding of musical elements in the recordings. *Select & Evaluate* 6. While presenting various recordings throughout the year, lead discussions about the different events and settings that feature live music, such as operas, musicals, recitals, and concerts. Discuss how the setting of each performance influences the type of music performed. 7. After listening and responding to several contrasting musical selections, give students a worksheet on which to select their favorite recordings. Lead a discussion about what their favorite pieces were, and why they were chosen. 8. Continuing the discussion about personal preference, play two contrasting recordings of the *same* piece of music. A good example is "Flight of the Bumblebee" by Rimsky-Korsakov, which has been transcribed for everything from tuba to choir. Discuss how the instrumental or vocal timbre changes the music.
Performance Assessment	Assess understanding of expressive elements through dramatic and movement exploration and performance. Use the included worksheets to assess analysis and the ability to express personal preference for listening examples.

Listening Evaluation Sheet

Third Grade

Name: _____   Date: _____

Class: _____

Write the name of the music being performed: _____

Was the music: *vocal*   *instrumental*   *both* ?

If you heard instruments, circle the families of instruments you heard:

    strings   *woodwinds*   *brass*   *percussion*

List at least one specific instrument that you heard: _____

What types of voices did you hear? _____

What was the main tempo (speed) of the performance? _____

What was the main dynamic (volume level) of the performance? _____

What was the mood of the performance? _____

What did the performers do well in the recording?

_____

_____

What did not go well in the performance?

_____

_____

Listening Selection Sheet

Third Grade

Name: _____   Date: _____

Class: _____

Below are listed most of the recorded pieces that we have listened to so far this year. Number the pieces from 1-4, with 1 being your favorite, or first choice, and 4 being your last choice.

_____   _____

_____   _____

In your own words, describe what you know about your #1 choice:

_____
_____
_____
_____

Write down why you chose this piece of music as your favorite:

_____
_____
_____
_____

As with the Performing process, we will allow fourth-grade and fifth-grade students more autonomy in actually selecting music to share. However, there are many lifetime's worth of quality recordings available, and we teachers should not cease to share these in order to broaden the experiences of our students. Rather, include your students' choices into the classroom discussion about the wide variety of musical styles.

	Responding Strand - Fourth Grade	
Grade/Class	Fourth Grade	
Date	Full Year	
Primary Elemental Objective	**Style**: Identify and discuss specific styles of music, such as symphonies and jazz music. Demonstrate personal preferences for specific pieces of music. Evaluate performances for quality and content.	
Secondary Elemental Objectives	**Melody, Rhythm, & Harmony**: Isolate specific patterns, scales, and/or harmonies, and use them as the basis for performance and improvisation.	
National/State Standards	**Core Music Standards:** MU:Re7.1.4 　*Demonstrate and explain how selected music connects to and is influenced by specific interests, experiences, purposes, or contexts.* MU:Re7.2.4 　*Demonstrate and explain how responses to music are informed by the structure, the use of the elements of music, and context (such as social and cultural).* MU:Re8.1.4 　*Demonstrate and explain how the expressive qualities (such as dynamics, tempo, and timbre) are used in performers' and personal interpretations to reflect expressive intent.* MU:Re9.1.4 　*Evaluate musical works and performances, applying established criteria, and explain appropriateness to the context.*	**21st Century Skills:** • Creativity & Innovation • Critical Thinking & Problem Solving • Communication & Collaboration • Flexibility & Adaptability • Initiative & Self-Direction • Productivity & Accountability • Leadership & Responsibility
Repertoire	"Finale" from Symphony #4 by P.I. Tchaikovsky "Allegro" from Symphony #5 by L.V. Beethoven "Duke's Place" by Duke Ellington Student-selected repertoire	
Media	Singing Barred Percussion or Recorder	Movement Drama

Responding Strand - Fourth Grade

Process **- Experience** **- Analyze** **- Create**	*Prior Knowledge & Skills* • Identify multiple musical elements in recorded music. • Be able to describe and discuss musical elements and personal preferences when listening to recorded music. *Analyze & Interpret* 1. Continue to play a variety of recordings of high-quality music for the class. Choose specific styles, cultures, ensembles, or time periods, and connect these choices with the rest of your curriculum. 2. Introduce the concept of the *symphony*, and play several examples, such as *Symphony #4* by P.I. Tchaikovsky. Play the "Finale" movement, and point out the folk song melody that is being used. If possible, reinforce the listening with reading and singing the tune. (see the folk song "Lovely Birch" in ***Xylophone & Other Barred Percussion***). 3. Another expressive symphonic example is the "Allegro" from Ludwig van Beethoven's *Symphony #5*. Discuss how the composer uses a simple, short repeated rhythmic pattern to create an entire movement. Identify dramatic elements such as dynamics and tempo, and discuss the resulting emotional impact of the work. Contrast with the second, slower "Andante" movement. 4. Diagram and discuss symphonic forms, using pieces such as those above. Identify the *allegro*, *theme & variations*, and *scherzo & trio* forms. 5. Continue using drama and/or dance to interpret recordings. 6. Introduce recordings of Jazz music, such as "Duke's Place" by Duke Ellington. Select specific elements such as the 12-bar blues form or the short melodic riff to teach and perform as a class. Use this melodic and harmonic material as the foundation for scat singing or instrumental improvisation. 7. Use worksheets such as those included to assess student understanding of musical elements in the recordings. *Select & Evaluate* 8. While presenting various recordings throughout the year, lead discussions about the different events and settings that feature live music, such as operas, musicals, recitals, and concerts. Discuss how the setting of each performance influences the type of music performed. Specifically compare and contrast a jazz band concert with a symphony concert, and discuss how the audience expectations differ. 9. After listening and responding to several contrasting musical selections, give students a worksheet on which to select their favorite recordings. Lead a discussion about what their favorite pieces are and why they were chosen. 10. Continuing the discussion about personal preference, play two contrasting recordings of the *same* piece of music. A good example is "Duke's Place," which is available in a wide variety of both instrumental and vocal arrangements. Discuss how the instrumental or vocal interpretation changes the music. 11. Give students the *Listening Proposal* worksheet included, and ask them to research a recording that they would like to share with the class. Allow time in class to visit a computer lab, or assign this as homework. This can be done as individuals or with partners. Once the worksheets are filled out, and recordings are previewed by you (to check for improper lyrics, for example), have each student or pair present the recording to the class, based on the information they gathered. Lead a class discussion about each piece and students' like i.e. dislike of the music. Guide students to give specific, musical reasons for their preferences.
Performance Assessment	Assess understanding of analyzed concepts through transferral to performance or improvisation. Assess ability to express personal preference and understanding of music through the included proposal worksheets and class presentations.

Listening Evaluation Sheet

Fourth Grade

Name: _____   Date: _____

Class: _____

Write the name of the music being performed: _____

Who was the composer? _____

Who is the performer or group? _____

What type of ensemble or group performed this piece? _____

Is this piece part of a larger work? _____ If yes, what is the larger work called?

_____

If you heard instruments, what type of ensemble (band, orchestra, choir, jazz band, etc.) did you hear? _____

What was the main tempo (speed) of the performance? _____

What was the main dynamic (volume level) of the performance? _____

What was the mood of the performance? _____

What is the *form* of this piece? _____

(worksheet continued on next page)

(4th Grade Listening Evaluation Sheet, p. 2)

What did the performers do well in the recording? Listen for balance, tuning, dynamics, etc.

_____
_____
_____
_____

What did not go well in the performance?

_____
_____
_____
_____

What was your favorite part of this recording?

_____
_____
_____
_____

What was your least favorite part of this recording?

_____
_____
_____
_____

Listening Proposal Sheet

Fourth Grade

Name: _____   Date: _____

Class: _____

Write down the title of a piece of music that *you* would like to listen to in class. Keep in mind that songs with explicit lyrics will *not* be chosen.

_____

Who is the performer and/or composer of this piece?

_____

In what year was this recording made?

_____

What is the style of this piece of music? How do you know?

_____

_____

_____

What is the meaning of the song/lyrics? What is it about?

_____

_____

_____

_____

(worksheet continued on next page)

(4th Grade Listening Proposal Sheet p. 2)

What can the class learn about music from this recording?

_____
_____
_____
_____

Why did you select this piece? What does it mean to you?

_____
_____
_____
_____

In addition to the widespread issue of focusing on *personal preferences* in the new standards, the transition from Fourth Grade Responding to Fifth Grade Responding introduces a new difficulty: the use of the phrase "citing evidence." These terms have been introduced to try to differentiate from one grade to the next. It is not easy, however, to comprehend the resulting meaning in practical terms. The best this author can assume is that MU:Re7.1.5 is asking students to show evidence of *how* a particular work is connected to an interest, experience, purpose, or context. MU:Re7.2.5 would then be asking students to show evidence of how their own or other's responses are influenced by musical elements and context.

	Responding Strand - Fifth Grade	
Grade/Class	Fifth Grade	
Date	Full Year	
Primary Elemental Objective	**Style**: Identify and discuss specific styles of music, such as suites and popular music. Demonstrate personal preferences for specific pieces of music. Evaluate performances for quality and content.	
Secondary Elemental Objectives	**Melody, Rhythm, & Harmony**: Isolate specific patterns, scales, and/or harmonies, and use them as the basis for performance and improvisation.	
National/State Standards	**Core Music Standards:** *MU:Re7.1.5* *Demonstrate and explain, citing evidence, how selected music connects to and is influenced by specific interests, experiences, purposes, or contexts.* *MU:Re7.2.5* *Demonstrate and explain, citing evidence, how responses to music are informed by the structure, the use of the elements of music, and context (such as social, cultural, and historical).* *MU:Re8.1.5* *Demonstrate and explain how the expressive qualities (such as dynamics, tempo, timbre, and articulation) are used in performers' and personal interpretations to reflect expressive intent.* *MU:Re9.1.5* *Evaluate musical works and performances, applying established criteria, and explain appropriateness to the context, citing evidence from the elements of music.*	**21st Century Skills:** • Creativity & Innovation • Critical Thinking & Problem Solving • Communication & Collaboration • Flexibility & Adaptability • Initiative & Self-Direction • Productivity & Accountability • Leadership & Responsibility
Repertoire	"Samba Lelê" by Barbatuques "Mars" from *The Planets* by Gustav Holst "Finale" from *Symphony #9* by Ludwig van Beethoven "Take Five" by Dave Brubeck	
Media	Recorder or Barred Percussion Singing	Drums

Responding Strand - Fifth Grade

Process **- Experience** **- Analyze** **- Create**	*Prior Knowledge & Skills* • Identify multiple musical elements in recorded music. • Be able to describe and discuss musical elements and personal preferences when listening to recorded music. *Analyze & Interpret* 1. Continue to play a variety of recordings of high-quality music for the class. Choose specific styles, cultures, ensembles, or time periods, and connect these choices with the rest of your curriculum. 2. Introduce new orchestral works, including symphonies, tone poems, and suites. Use the "Finale" from *Symphony #9* by Beethoven as an example of how early Romantic composers broke the simple forms and rules of earlier Classical symphonies. In this work, Beethoven stretches the form and adds solo and choral singers. Discuss Beethoven's deafness, and the impact this would have had on his writing and conducting of such a work. Sing or play the "Ode to Joy" theme from the "Finale." 3. Another work for orchestra to introduce is *The Planets* by Gustav Holst. Explore how this suite differs from a symphony in structure, and share that the thematic material for each movement was based on the astrological signs associated with each planet. Have students read and perform the ostinato rhythm from "Mars" on drums or other unpitched percussion. 4. Diagram and discuss symphonic forms using pieces such as those above. Identify the *allegro*, *theme & variations*, and *scherzo & trio* forms. 5. Continue presenting recordings of Jazz music, such as "Take Five" by Dave Brubeck. Identify and discuss the odd 5/4 meter. Select an element, such as the piano ostinato, to transfer to barred percussion. Use this as a springboard for continued exploration of scat singing and/or instrumental improvisation. 6. Use worksheets such as those included to assess student understanding of musical elements in the recordings. *Select & Evaluate* 7. While presenting various recordings throughout the year, continue to discuss the different events and settings that feature live music, such as operas, musicals, recitals, and concerts. Discuss how the setting of each performance influences the type of music performed. 8. After listening and responding to several contrasting musical selections, give students a worksheet on which to select their favorite recordings. Lead a discussion about what their favorite pieces are and why they were chosen. 9. Continuing the discussion about personal preference, play two contrasting recordings of the *same* piece of music. Discuss how the performers' interpretation changes the music. 10. Introduce new and exciting modern music from around the world, such as "Samba Lelê" by Barbatuques. Use as the springboard for students to discuss their own personal tastes in music, and also as a motivation to learn new works for performance. 11. Give students the *Listening Proposal* worksheet included, and ask them to research a recording that they would like to share with the class. Allow time in class to visit a computer lab, or assign this as homework. This can be done as individuals or with partners. Once the worksheets are filled out, and recordings are previewed by you (to check for improper lyrics, for example), have each student or pair present the recording to the class, based on the information they gathered. Lead a class discussion about each piece and students' like or dislike for the music. Guide students to give specific, musical reasons for their preferences.
Performance Assessment	Assess understanding of analyzed concepts through transferral to performance or improvisation. Assess ability to express personal preference and understanding of music through the included proposal worksheets and class presentations.

Listening Evaluation Sheet

Fifth Grade

Name: _____   Date: _____

Class: _____

Write the name of the music being performed: _____

Who was the composer? _____

Who is the performer or group? _____

What type of ensemble or group performed this piece? _____

Is this piece part of a larger work? _____ If yes, what is the larger work called?

_____

If you heard instruments, what type of ensemble did you hear? _____

What was the main tempo (speed) of the performance? _____

What was the main dynamic (volume level) of the performance? _____

What was the mood of the performance? _____

What is the *form* of this piece? _____

What was the purpose or function of this piece? How do you know?

_____
_____
_____

(worksheet continued on next page)

(5th Grade Listening Evaluation Sheet, p. 2)

What did the performers do well in the recording? Listen for balance, tuning, dynamics, etc.

_____
_____
_____
_____

What did not go well in the performance?

_____
_____
_____
_____

What was your favorite part of this recording?

_____
_____
_____
_____

What was your least favorite part of this recording?

_____
_____
_____
_____

Listening Proposal Sheet

Fifth Grade

Name: _____ Date: _____

Class: _____

Write down the title of a piece of music that *you* would like to listen to in class. Keep in mind that songs with explicit lyrics will *not* be chosen.

_____

Who is the performer and/or composer of this piece?

_____

In what year was this recording made?

_____

What is the style of this piece of music? How do you know?

_____
_____
_____

What is the meaning of the song/lyrics? What is it about?

_____
_____
_____
_____

(worksheet continued on next page)

5th Grade Listening Proposal Sheet p. 2)

Why was this piece written and performed? How do you know?

_____
_____
_____
_____
_____

What can the class learn about music from this recording? How does it relate, compare, or contrast with other recordings from class?

_____
_____
_____
_____
_____
_____
_____

Why did you select this piece? What does it mean to you?

_____
_____
_____
_____
_____
_____
_____

Artistic Process: Connecting

The Connecting Process is deeply embedded in all we do as creative elementary music teachers. By performing folk music and listening to historical recordings, we celebrate and engage in discussions about culture, history, and society. The new *selecting* and *imagining* Process Components in Creating, Performing, and Responding ask students to use and discuss personal knowledge when interacting with music in the classroom. For this reason, a well-balanced program following the new Core Standards has no need for specific lessons written solely for the purpose of connecting. Rather, these standards have been integrated into the lessons in the previous three chapters, as they will be with your own class.

Practical Application

Accommodating Reflective Practice

According to the new standards, students must not only possess musical knowledge and perform and create competently, they must also be able to explain their processes, reactions, and decisions. While this is certainly an important part of deep understanding of any subject area, the challenge lies in the time required to reflect, discuss, and assess such processes.

There are basically three ways that students can express their thinking in music class.

- *Writing*: Students can write a goal statement before a project, document the process during a project, or write a reflection at the end of a project or each step in a project.

- *Discussion*: Students can share ideas verbally with a partner, the teacher, a small group, or the class.

- *Non-verbal communication*: Students can demonstrate understanding through a chosen form of non-verbal communication, such as movement, drawing, or improvising an accompaniment or harmony.

Writing

In the elementary general music classroom, there are several obstacles to written work. Many rooms are arranged with music-making as the priority. Therefore, such rooms often have no desks, an open space for movement and games, and a variety of instruments organized in different areas. Students often sit on the floor when they are not active. In order to perform a writing activity, students must have a had surface, such as a book, dry-erase board, or clipboard. Pencils or other writing devices and paper must be passed out. All of this must then be collected again before the class can move on to a different activity.

Writing is also a time-intensive activity for students, especially in the lower grades, or for students with learning disabilities. In fact, many students have IEP plans that require teachers to give those students extra time, to allow them to dictate their ideas to a teacher or aide, or to let them use a computer to type. It may be that you are unaware of these accommodations and needs to look into such issues before starting a written assignment. Even non-IEP students need adequate time to formulate ideas and present them in a written format.

Some strategies for minimizing the time involved in writing tasks include giving multiple-choice questions, using manipulatives or graphic notation instead of standard notation to represent and document a musical idea, or using technology, such as a classroom digital voting system[4]. Students can also work with partners or in small groups, but you must take care to ensure that every child is part of the thinking and writing process.

Discussion

Unlike writing, discussion requires no specific setup. It is helpful to have a room in which everyone can be easily heard, and arranging students in a circle or semicircle can facilitate better eye contact and engagement. Discussion can happen at any point during a lesson, although students with instruments or other objects in their hands will be less successful at focusing than those who are sitting without distractions.

There are two difficulties with discussion. The first is that outgoing, verbal students tend to dominate the discussion, while quieter students tend to be left out. You must make sure to call on every student, not always starting with the ones who raise their hands quickly, and an expectation of response must be established early on. The other challenge is that in order for everyone to be heard, a discussion in a class of thirty students can take up even more time than completing a worksheet.

---

[4] ActiVote by Promethean is one such example.
http://www.prometheanworld.com/us/english/education/products/assessment-and-student-response/activote/

One strategy to combat this problem is to start with partners or very small groups. Insist that each student takes a turn to talk in his/her group, then have the small groups combine into larger groups and share a summary of their previous discussion. Groups can be combined multiple times until the entire class is in one group. While this does not allow the teacher to hear each student, it does encourage more participation than your simply calling on a few students to speak.

Non-verbal Communication

As creative music educators, we often think of *responding* in terms of moving to music. Dance and drama can be key ways for students to demonstrate their understanding of a musical concept without words. There are several examples of this in the *Responding* chapter. These activities mirror the *Creating* Process, and create a connection to Dance standards, which unfortunately are not fully taught in most of our schools. Likewise, students who sing or play along with a recording are demonstrating awareness of the melody, rhythm, tempo, and form. Drawing also allows students to interpret what they are listening to creatively with yet another art form.

Connecting the Artistic Processes

In many traditional Orff Schulwerk or **Creative Sequence** lessons, experience precedes exploration and improvisation. Concepts that are learned through performance are then explored, broken apart, and reassembled into new musical ideas. This is a logical, sequential approach that develops understanding through multiple applications of a single musical concept. Unfortunately, the new Core Standards do not draw clear connections between the Performing and Creating Processes; instead, they appear to be isolated from each other. Nevertheless, it is imperative that teachers make these connections, and do not try to teach improvisation or composition based on unfamiliar skills.

The Responding Process can and should also be tied directly into Perfoming and Creating lessons. Students will be more engaged to listen to music that they have performed, and will be more informed to perform music that they have studied through listening. Likewise, listening to jazz musicians is a key activity for teaching students to improvise.

Focusing on Skills and Elements

A well-balanced curriculum will *not* give equal weight or time to each Process Component in the new Core Standards. Rather, those components that emphasize the development of musical skills and knowledge of musical elements *must* be treated as the primary responsibility of you, the music educator. Selecting, responding, and discussing can only be taught to developing musicians, not to students who lack musical training.

Coda

The new National Core Arts Standards have truly changed the discussion about music education in this country. It is a bold document that seeks to re-envision our profession and the experiences of our students. As a veteran teacher and teacher educator, I do not view all of these changes as positive. I hope that the dialogue continues as we search for meaning in these new standards. I am concerned that beginning teachers will read the document literally and create a discussion-rich curriculum that fails to teach students lifelong music skills.

It is the job of all of us, especially experienced teachers, to be a part of this discussion. Write a blog about your experiences with the new standards, hold a discussion group in your local Orff or Kodaly chapter, go to a conference, or send an email to NAfME. Test pilot the new Cornerstone Assessments or the lessons in this book. Advocate in your state for *adapting*, not simply *adopting* the new standards. Work locally, statewide, and nationally to sustain and grow music as a vital part of every child's education. If you want to share your experiences with me, I would be happy to post them to my blog at timpurdum.com.

I hope these lessons have helped you begin to understand the new Core Standards. I also hope they fit seamlessly into your existing **Creative Sequence**. Wishing every one of you the best for you and your students,

Tim Purdum

tim@cedarrivermusic.com

Selected Bibliography

Books

Erdei, Ida, Faith Knowles, & Denise Bacon, ed. *My Singing Bird: 150 Folk Songs*. Bexley, OH: Kodály Center of America, 2002. Print.

Erdei, Peter, ed. *150 American Folk Songs to sing, read, and play.* New York: Boosey & Hawkes, 2004. Print.

Goodkin, Doug. *Now's the Time: Teaching Jazz to All Ages*. San Francisco: Pentatonic Press, 2004. Print.

Keetman, Gunild and Carl Orff. *Music for Children, Volumes 1-IV*. Ed. Margaret Murray. Mainz, Germany: Schott, 1976. Print.

Keetman, Gunild. *Spielbuch für Xylophon, Band I*. Mainz, Germany: Schott, 1965. Print.

Locke, Eleanor, ed. *Sail Away: 155 American Folk Songs to sing, read, and play.* New York: Boosey & Hawkes, 1981. Print.

López-Ibor, Sofia and Verena Maschat. *¡Quien canta su mal espanta! Singing Drives away Sorrow! Songs, Games, and Dances from Latin America.* Mainz, Germany: Schott, 2006. Print.

Purdum, Tim. *Creative Sequence: Teaching Music with Flexibility & Organization.* Cedar Falls, IA: Cedar River Music, 2012. Print.

Steen, Arvida. *Exploring Orff: A Teacher's Guide.* Mainz, Germany: Schott, 1992. Print.

Wright, Blanche Fisher. *The Real Mother Goose*. Fairless Hills, PA: Checkerboard Press, 1944. Print.

Websites

The Kodaly Center. The American Folk Song Collection. Holy Names University. Web. 10 Oct. 2014. <http://kodaly.hnu.edu>

American Orff Schulwerk Association. 2014. Web. 10 Oct. 2014. <http://www.aosa.org>

American Recorder Society. 2013. Web. 10 Oct. 2014. <http://americanrecorder.org>

Lander, Nicholas S. The Recorder Homepage. Web. 10 Oct. 2014. <http://www.recorderhomepage.net>

National Core Standards for Arts Education. State Education Agency Directors of Art Education (SEADAE), 2014. Web. 10 Oct. 2014. <http://nationalartsstandards.org>

National Association for Music Education (NAfME). Web. 10 Oct. 2014. <http://nafme.org>

Purdum, Tim. Creative Sequence Online. Cedar River Music, 2012. Web. 10 Oct. 2014. <http://cs.cedarrivermusic.com>

Purdum, Tim. Tim Purdum: Music, Movement, and Curriculum Specialist. Blog. 10 Oct. 2014. <http://timpurdum.com>

Recordings[5]

Barbatuques. "Samba Lelê." *Tum Pá*. MCD, 2012. iTunes.

Beethoven, Ludwig van. "Allegro" from *Symphony #5*. *Beethoven Live at the Proms*. BBC Scottish Symphony Orchestra. BBC Music, 1997. CD.

Beethoven, Ludwig van. "Finale: Presto" from *Symphony No. 9 in D Minor*. *The Best of Beethoven*. Naxos, 1997. CD.

Brubeck, Dave. "Take Five." *The Essential Dave Brubeck*. Sony, 2003. iTunes.

---

[5] The recordings listed here represent the author's personal collection. Feel free to substitute or compare any other quality recording for each piece. Many works can also be found at youtube.com or downloaded from iTunes or Amazon.

Ellington, Duke. "Duke's Place."

Grieg, Edvard. "IV: In the Hall of the Mountain King" from *Peer Gynt Suite*. *The 50 Most Essential Pieces of Classical Music*. London Philharmonic Orchestra. X5 Music, 2008. iTunes.

Haydn, Franz Joseph. "Andante (Surprise)" from *Symphony #94 in G*. *The Best of Naxos 7*. Naxos, 1993. CD.

Holst, Gustav. *The Planets*. Chicago Symphony Orchestra. Deutsch Grammophon, 1989. CD.

Humperdinck, Engelbert. *Hansel and Gretel - A Fairytale Opera in 3 Acts*. Andreas Delfs and the Milwaukee Symphony Orchestra. Avie, 2008. iTunes.

Mozart, Wolfgang Amadeus. "12 Variations on 'Ah Vous Dirai-je Maman.'" *Complete Variations and Other Works for Solo Piano*. Walter Klein. Musical Concepts, 2007. iTunes.

Mozart, Wolfgang Amadeus. *Die Zauberflöte (The Magic Flute)*. London Philharmonic Orchestra. Chandos, 2005. iTunes.

Orff, Carl. "O Fortuna" *Carmina Burana*. London Symphony Chorus, London Symphony Orchestra. LSO, 2005. iTunes.

Orff, Carl and Gunild Keetman. "Street Song (Gassenhäuer)." *Musica Poetica: Orff-Schulwerk* (Disc 1). Celestial Harmonies, 1995. CD.

Rachmaninoff, Sergei. "The Flight of the Bumble-Bee" from *The Tale of Tsar Saltan*. *Rachmaninov Plays Rachmaninov*. Decca, 1979. iTunes.

Rodgers, Richard and Oscar Hammerstein. *The Sound of Music*. 20th Century Fox, 1965. Amazon Instant Video.

Rossini, Gioachino. "Overture" from *William Tell*. *Rossini/Shostakovich*. The Philadelphia Orchestra, 2005. iTunes.

Saint-Saëns, Camille. *Carnival of the Animals*. *Saint-Saëns: Carnival of the Animals, Bizet: Jeux d'enfants, & Ravel: Mother Goose*. London Symphony Orchestra, 2005. CD.

Saint-Saëns, Camille. *Danse Macabre*. *Saint-Saens: Symphony No.3 "Organ"; Bacchanale from "Samson et Dalila"; Prélude from "Le Déluge"; Danse macabre*. Chicago Symphony Orchestra. Deutsche Grammophon, 2003. iTunes.

Shenanigans. "Carnivalito - Bolivian." *Bush Dances of New Holland, The Best of Shenanigans, Vol. 2*. Shenanigans, 1994. CD.

Shostakovich, Dimitri. *Peter and the Wolf*. *Prokofiev: Peter and the Wolf, Lieutenant Kije Symphonic Suite*. Boris Karloff, Mario Rossi, & Wiener Opernorchester. IndieBlu Music, 2009. iTunes.

Sousa, John Phillip. "Stars and Stripes Forever." *Sousa II*. US Marine Band. Altissimo, 1998. iTunes.

Tchaikovsky, Pyotr Il'yich. "Finale" from *Symphony #4. Tchaikovsky: Symphony No. 4 & Romeo and Juliet*. Daniel Barenboim & Chicago Symphony Orchestra. Warner Classics, 1997. CD.

Tchaikovsky, Piotr Il'yich. *The Nutcracker (Complete Ballet Score)*. Royal Philharmonic Orchestra, 1995. iTunes.

www.ingramcontent.com/pod-product-compliance
Lightning Source LLC
Chambersburg PA
CBHW041537220426
43663CB00002B/57